Freedom Clause
14 Amendments to Freedom

Colby Sutter

Freedom Clause: 14 Amendments to Freedom

CrossLink Publishing
www.crosslinkpublishing.com

ISBN 978-1-63357-019-1

Library of Congress Control Number: 2015930115

Dedication

I dedicate this book to my Lord and Savior Jesus Christ and in memory of the three queens who raised me: my mom, Linsley Bedell Sutter, my heart and soul, my earth, the one who kept me grounded and inspired throughout my life, my best friend, who, on her deathbed, looked at me and said, "I see the book you will one day write, and it is beautiful"; my grandma Mary Bedell, the leader of the family, the one who taught us all about Jesus and the importance of the Bible; and my aunt Holly Ferstler, the walking example in my life of grace and love. These three ladies always smiled; they were always filled with joy and the word of God. My three queens showed me how to live like a saint and how to die with a smile like an angel. You will be forever missed and never forgotten. And like my mom told me before she passed, "I am in your future, not your past. I will be right around the corner waiting for you, cheering you on."

Also, this book is dedicated to my beautiful fiancée, Johanna Shuster, who supported me and stood by my side as I followed my dreams. You're my anchor.

Thank-You Page

I just want to thank a few people without whom this book would have never been written.

My favorite brother, Chris, and his wife Amy Sutter for always standing by my side. I would lay my life down for you guys. Johanna Shuster, Pastor John and Lisa Carter for being not only mentors and teachers but also family, and Uncle B.J. and the entire Bedell family. Monica Richardson for helping me edit the book, Pastor Carl and Jeanne Bargabos for being the best second set of parents a person could ask for, Gary (the man) Crisalli, Aaron Harris, Elder Hank and Pastor Angela Perry for showing me what love is all about, Pastor Harry, Chris Newkirk, Rich Longden, Brandi Rooker, Andy Sanders, Tommy Elleman Jr., Pastor Joe Coudriet, Josh Del Favero, Pastor Lee Wilson, Pastor Lee Williams, Pastor Piper for trying to fix me, my doctor Adam Peddock, my trainer Nick Murphy, and my life coach Angela Douglas, who made me set writing goals to finish this book.

ABOUT THE AUTHOR

Colby Sutter is the founder and director of Seven Miles Ministry, established in 2012. The name Seven Miles originated from a concept that means life can be like a seven-mile walk (Luke 24:13–35), for in order to change someone's life, you need to walk the entire seven miles with them. Hence, the tagline: "Changing the World One Step at a Time." Its mission is simple—to set people free from bondage, addiction, pain, defeat, lack of love, hopelessness, and lifelessness through motivational testimony, education, understanding, and love. To contact Colby Sutter for speaking engagements or questions, please visit the Seven Mile website *www.sevenmiles.org* or e-mail the author at *Colby@sevenmiles.org*.

The author most recently worked in several severely troubled Syracuse, New York, inner-city schools as a program manager. During this time, he also developed, implemented, and coordinated the continued success of his own programs, which has been noted for improving the dropout rate in the Syracuse City school district.

He has served as the gambling prevention coordinator for Prevention Network, as well as the program coordinator for youth development. His expertise is specifically on drugs and drug addiction. He has taught numerous classes for NYS on drug education, addiction, and gambling prevention. He has been asked on many occasions to appear on the local news as a drug expert. Professionally and personally, he has researched the dangers of addiction, producing papers and providing documentation that has been cited by local media. He has spent a great deal of time as a facilitator for those enrolled in a certified training program to become credentialed alcoholism and substance abuse counselors. Additional experience includes working for the County of Oswego Council on Alcoholism as well as participating in speaking engagements throughout the Northeast.

Moreover, he has a strong background in criminal justice, working for five years as the assistant director at a federal reentry center for inmates and attending graduate school for criminal justice administration. He has spent several years working with troubled youth at Elmcrest Children's Center, as well as various youth groups and mission activities through his local church and with Syracuse-based organizations, such as the Rescue Mission and Teen Challenge. He currently works as the director of youth ministries, youth pastor, and Sunday school superintendent for a local church in Syracuse.

His years spent working in juvenile justice and correctional institutions have softened his heart to those impacted by this epidemic. He has spoken to thousands of adults and teens about the dangers of drug and alcohol abuse. Statistics show that every person is touched by drugs in some way, directly or indirectly. It's his passion to bring the wisdom he's gained on these issues to the world.

Colby Sutter is engaged to be married to the love of his life, Johanna Shuster, on October 17, 2015. He loves Jesus, reading and studying the Bible, boxing, football, and his family.

Contents

Chapter One
Introduction

I remember the first time I felt hopeless, unloved, and alone. I remember the first time I tried to commit suicide; I was eight years old—eight years old and filled with pain. Perhaps you can trace your pain far back or even further. Maybe you, too, have felt or feel hopeless, spending sleepless night after sleepless night screaming out to God to take your pain away, to take away your horror, to once again fill you with joy. Maybe you have a desire to smile again, smile a "real" smile—a smile that is not forced, a smile that you don't just put on so people won't see the real you, see the pain and hopelessness in your face. This book is meant to be a guide to the blind, a light to those who are in darkness. It will give you hope. It will give you the tools to be set free from anything you are facing. This book will get you closer to God. God has a purpose for all of us. This book will help you find that purpose so you can live out the calling God has for you. This book is about the true meaning of freedom. "And you will know the truth, and the truth will set you free" (John 8:32).

The one thing I have learned in life is this: if you want to change anything—your habits, behaviors, addictions, sexual desires, devotional time with God, anything at all you want to change—you must ask for strength and help from God, and he will give them to you. He will also give the steps that you must follow. He will direct your way, but you must choose to walk that path.

I have spoken at hundreds of speaking engagements, and during this time I have noticed a common theme. Most people who are hurting—I mean, truly hurting—the ones who feel hopeless, who think there are no other options in life, who are suicidal, who turn to drugs for relief or to escape their pain, these people are not much different than the people who think they have it all together, who walk the walk and talk the talk in life. If you sit down and speak to anyone of them, you will notice that their childhood shaped their beliefs about who they are and what they could become. The experiences they went through while growing up determine the way they see themselves and are also greatly linked to their feelings of hopelessness and sense of worth. I remember speaking at a school to a group of about fifty so-called "troubled students." I was there to address a drug problem the school was going through. In my spirit, I sensed that this was going to be an amazing time, so I prayed and prayed on what to do for this presentation. The Lord told me to go in and sit with them and talk; no PowerPoint, no notes, just sit with them and talk to them, show them I care for them. I did and the result was amazing! Kids were crying, asking how to change and how to get help.

One girl told me, "My dad says I'm worthless every day and that I will be a loser forever, so why shouldn't I do drugs?"

Another young man told me, "My family does drugs. My friends do drugs. We have no other choices in this society; we might as well do drugs."

Another student told me how his dad would beat him. He would call for his mom to save him, but she would be too high on heroin to do anything. I had girls and guys telling me about their suicide attempts, showing me scars from where they'd cut themselves. I never once told them my story or how I could relate. I just listened and I cared. I cried with the students, laughed with them, gave them information about drugs and drug abuse, but never lectured them into feeling guilty about how they saw themselves. Every kid would use the word "worthless" and "helpless" while describing themselves or their situation. God used me that day like I would never imagine. I ministered to those kids and I saw change. I could not say "God" because it was a public school, but I offered steps, the fourteen steps of freedom that God has given me. I showed them how to implement them, change their way of thinking, and have hope. These steps did work! But this is what blew me away: the teachers saw such a difference in the students that the school asked me if I could come back every month to talk to the kids, work with them, and keep them on track. These kids made a pledge to stop doing drugs on their own volition. They signed it and hung it up at the school. They made a change and decided not to be like their parents, not to let what happened in their childhood determine who they were going to be in life. One girl gave me a card, and it said, "Thank you for giving me hope in what I thought was a hopeless life. You saved my life."

So now I am going to share these same steps (I will be calling them "amendments") with you. They will work if you will allow them to work in your life. You, too, can change your circumstances; you can change what you thought about your destiny.

Before we begin, I need you to understand where I come from, so I am going to tell you a little bit about my childhood and teenage years. Later, we'll talk about my life as a young adult—this is where my life really got interesting, where things began to fall apart. But before we discuss the destruction, let's go back to the beginning.

I never told anyone about this story until now. At eight years old, I sat on my parents' bed, took a CO_2 pellet pistol gun, put one pellet in it, spun the chamber around, put the barrel of the gun in my mouth, closed my lips around it, and, with eyes full of tears, I pulled the trigger. I did not do it for attention. I did it because the pain inside, even at eight, was already unbearable. I was already imprisoned with pain needing to be set free. I already did not feel loved. I thank God the pellet did not come out; I thank God that it was *only* a pellet gun. At that age, I didn't know any better. I thought that type of gun would kill me, but looking back now, it would have just been very painful and hard to explain to a doctor how a pellet got embedded into the back of my mouth. This is just one of the many situations of my childhood that helped shape me. But there's more.

I remember my dad calling me retarded, worthless—things like that. The first time I remember him hitting me was when I was in kindergarten; he took a metal part of his belt and struck me across the face with it. It's amazing I cannot remember what I did wrong, but I can remember the beating I got. I remember my first fight, also in kindergarten. I was wearing a green sweater that I hated. A kid made fun of it, and I rapidly smashed his head into the cold brick wall of the school. I remember my older brother getting thrown down the stairs. I remember him getting his head smashed through our hallway wall. I remember having my head wrapped up in a blanket as my dad put his full body weight on me.

I screamed for help, saying, "I can't breathe."

And he would laugh at me, saying, "If you can cry, you can breathe."

This would be his method of "calming me down" whenever I'd lose my temper. At age seven, I caught my dad cheating on my mom. He told me it was nothing, and then said, "Do not say anything." By age twelve, my parents sat me down and told me they were getting a divorce, shortly after my dad took off. Now here I was, a young teen filled with so much hatred, pain, and anger. We started to move around and switch schools. My mom was working all the time. I learned fast that you are never safe in this world; tragedy can happen to you, not just to "other people."

During the first move, I got jumped by a bunch of kids in this new city on my first week. Alone and with no friends yet, I lashed back at them one by one when I saw them. This turned into a year of looking over my shoulder, never feeling safe, and hating where I live. The next place we moved into, I was with a group of people I just met, my new friends. So I thought. I got jumped by ten kids, and all my so-called "friends" took off running, leaving me alone. This time I was a little older, and this time it hurt a lot more. I realized fast that the only one going to take care of me was me. This became my mantra. Someone looks at you wrong, attack them. Someone insults you, attack them. You want something, take it. You need money, get it by any means necessary because nobody else will ever help you. Everyone will leave you in the end. I started to carry weapons with me—guns, knives, brass knuckles—anything I could find. Fighting was the only way I knew to cope with the pain of this feeling of being alone, not loved, this feeling of death inside. Besides fighting, I would eventually find another method of escape—drugs.

By seventh grade, I was drinking regularly and smoking weed and cigarettes. This was also the year I started failing classes; summer schools started to become a regular thing. Now, when I was a kid, it was almost unheard of for a middle schooler to drink and use drugs. Nowadays, it seems to be the norm. When you start doing drugs young, it moves fast, almost like an aggressive cancer. Soon, you become bored and need new things to entertain you; it opens doors to other drugs. In eighth grade, I got in a fight with two kids. I got hit from the side that tore all the cartilage in my knee. I needed an operation and physical therapy, but I also got this wonderful thing called pain pills. They became my daily vitamins. I would take them every day all the way until my senior year in high school, because the doctor just kept refilling my script when I told him I was still in pain. (He eventually lost his practice.) I also started stealing, breaking into cars and houses. I even started to rob people just to feel that power and control my dad took away from me. It made me feel untouchable. There was no greater "high" than being feared and respected. High school opened up other doors of opportunity for me, and it brought other ways to bury the pain deep down inside. This pain often left me crying for death, crying for any kind of relief. It caused me to live a double life. Most people saw me as a funny jokester in school, but the "real" me would do drugs alone in my room at night or with a few select friends.

In ninth grade, I tried steroids, coke, and acid. But what I found out was that I could sell drugs and really feel important, needed, and loved. This would change my life. The feeling I got from selling drugs was beyond words. For the first time in my life, I felt in control and important. People needed me. They would seek me out, call me, invite me to parties, and want what I have. Once again, I was living a double life. Only a select few knew I sold drugs in high school; the others saw my fake smile and laugh. This led me to need different rushes to get excited. I started to break into stores at night while they were closed, stealing alcohol and sometimes even money if they left it in the register. In and out fast, with the getaway car waiting. Or sometimes we even stayed a few hours in the place we broke into and partied. I even got so cocky at one time that I walked into a store in the middle of the day, grabbed two cases of beer, and just walked right out. Too bad the cashier knew who I was, and the owner of the store was a local judge. Needless to say, that did not work out well for me. I was also in ninth grade when I pulled my first gun on someone. I was walking with a group of friends, and my brother drove by to pick us up. As he did, this group of fortysomething men sitting outside drinking beer started to throw rocks at his car. So I walked over to them, asking if they had a problem. They began to yell back and walked toward me. This time my "friends" stood by my side. I pulled up my shirt, showing my gun in my waist, and said, "Who wants to make a move?" The guys all turned around. Although I felt respected and people feared me, the truth was that inside I felt worse and worse, and the pain grew. I thought of death every night. I wanted to die but was scared to kill myself. Let me take that back. I did not *truly* want to die; I wanted the pain to go away. And death seemed to be the only way out. This was the first time I took a razor and cut myself. I never told anyone or showed anyone. This was my secret way of releasing the pain I had deep down inside of me. The cuts would slowly allow me to breathe and taste freedom. Soon, life just became one big suicidal thought after another; pain seemed to be in every corner where I lived. The way I was living was building up my character and making me turn into a person who deep down I really wasn't.

At this point in my life, the police were very familiar with me. By the time I reached tenth grade, I had girls stealing for me. I would have them go into local stores. I would give them a list, and they would come out with the items on the list. I remember one time when we all stole 40s (beer) from a store. As we turned the corner, there was a policeman and an undercover loss prevention associate. We all took off, running in different directions. I was the only one smart enough to toss my 40s behind some chips in the isle as I was running. All my friends got caught. I got caught in the parking lot making my way to the car. They brought us all back into the store. Everyone was getting in trouble for stealing except me, because I tossed mine. They tried to get me to admit I had taken something, but I did not. I got to leave as all my friends got in trouble. Things kept getting worse grade after grade.

By the time eleventh grade came along, I was giving my poor single mother a hard time every day. My best friend and I stole his dad's car. While driving this car to a party, we decided to smoke weed and drink Jack Daniels right out of the bottle. I vividly remember taking the bottle of whiskey right to my lips and chugging as I saw flashing lights bouncing around the inside of our car. I looked over to my buddy, who was driving, and saw the panic in his face as he was pulling over. Now what I remember most about this incident is that the police already knew who I was. As they approached the car, they said, "Colby, please get out of the car and put your hands on your head." As I did, I remember dropping a bag of weed very carefully into the grass. We got caught for the stolen car and the alcohol, but they did not find the weed. I also remember the disappointment in my mom's face when she came to pick me up at the police station at three in the morning.

Eleventh grade was rough. My best friend since eighth grade got in a fight at school with a kid whom other students had paid to beat him up. We started to walk up to this kid, and then my buddy just attacked him. I did nothing but watch. My best friend ended up breaking the kid's eye socket, nose, and jaw. He left him lying lifeless in the parking lot. We then ran to my car and drove away. An eyewitness would later say that we jumped on the kid and that I was involved. I was not. But having the reputation that I'd been developing over the years, it was easy for people to think I was involved. My best friend and I got arrested. After questioning from the police and from the school, I was let go. I did not say a word. My best friend turned himself in and admitted everything. He ended up getting four years in prison, got kicked out of school, and got sued. His mom lost everything she had.

I came home from school one day to find my mom sitting on her bed with a duffle bag of mine. In that duffle bag were mass quantities of drugs I was selling; she had them all dumped out on her bed. I was expecting to get yelled at, screamed at, but no, all she did was cry. (I will never forget this as long as I live.) With a face full of tears, she looked me in the eyes and questioned, "Colby, how did I fail you as a mother?" She then asked me if I needed help—*if I needed help?*—and not what I was doing with my life. She loved me so much that all she cared about was her little boy. It felt like I just got punched in the gut by a sledgehammer. I remember crying and telling her I would change. Just for her I would change, I promised her. I loved my mom so much that I could not bear to see her in pain. I had to fix the pain and I did. I stopped everything. I even stopped drinking. I became a person who didn't sell or take drugs and didn't even drink. I wish my story ended there, but it didn't. This is actually where my story starts. Those were of my good days, the days before things got really bad. If you can imagine that.

I turned my life around for a short period of time, long enough to go to college and get a 4.0, president's list, and honor society. After college was when I really started to sell drugs; got involved in organized crime; hurt people so badly that I still cannot talk about it; had death on my hands; begged God to kill me; and lost everyone and things I loved. I hated myself. While trying to get involved in the local church, I was looking at prison time.

I was so lost. I had so much pain and anger that I could not feel anything else. I did not feel God's love. But everything was hidden behind a fake smile. I was volunteering at the church. I was speaking at church events about my life. I was being invited at other churches as the main speaker at conferences, talking about my life. But I still felt lost.

Finally, after two years of walking with God in every aspect of my life, I cried out to him and asked him to fix me, to give me something that would take the pain away. I just wanted to feel joy again. I would do anything to feel joy and be happy again. The Lord answered me and gave me a process—steps to take to be set free from any kind of bondages we face in life, to bring us to the next level in our Christian walk. No matter where you are in your journey with God, this book will help you get to the next level of freedom and love that the Lord wants you to have. I will give you the steps (amendments) He gave to me. I will also give you real examples from my life. I will also give you rules to follow for each step (amendment), so you can implement them into your life long term. I will back up each rule with scriptures.

This Is My Vision of this Book

During the worst part of my life, I finally made a change to become a Christian, but not just a Christian. I made a choice to go "all in" to become the best Christian I could be. What I noticed is that I would praise and worship God, yet inside I was miserable. I would go home and be depressed. I didn't feel forgiven. I didn't feel loved. I was incapable of feeling anything except anger. I felt hopeless. People would say things like, "The love of God will change you. His presence will set you free. You just need to push in." I did; I pushed in and nothing. I was still angry and miserable. I just hid it deeper. Finally, God gave me fourteen steps that would change my life and set me free—fourteen steps (amendments) of freedom that gave me hope for the first time in my life. I became motivated to develop a guidebook to give hope back to the hopeless, to wake up and give life back to the people who have died inside.

This book is for a Christian who suffers from defeat, misery, pain, lack of support, and/or addictions—anything and everything that is holding him or her back in life. This is for the person who is trying to be the best he or she can be. The one going to church, praying, and reading the Bible, but for some reason he or she still cannot make that breakthrough and feel free. He or she is still miserable. Inside, he or she is spiritually dead. This is for the Christian who hears the Word, hears about God's love, yet deep down inside there is emptiness, hatred, pain, and anger. I have seen so many Christians who put on this act in life. They try to show that everything is fine, that they are happy and full of joy, and that God is moving in their lives. Then after ministering to them, they start to tell me about sexual addiction, adultery, anger, and so many other things that they just cannot break free from. This breaks my heart. In the body of Christ, people are hurting, His people are hurting. Oftentimes, the ones who seem to have it all together are the ones hurting the most. At times they feel as though death is their only way of escape. Death seems to be the freedom. This is for any Christian at any level in the faith who just wants to get closer to God. Through this book and the Holy Spirit, which give hope to the hopeless, I believe that people will experience a new life.

If you truly desire freedom, change, joy, hope, peace, and love, I encourage you to keep reading this book. Now let's pray.

Father:

I thank you for today. I thank you, for you woke me up this morning. I ask that you forgive me of my sins, Father God. I ask that you bless my hands as I write this. I ask that you fill me with your spirit, Lord, so whoever reads this book will be blessed and become free from whatever circumstances they are facing in life. I ask that this book would change lives, help people get closer to you, and be set free from suffering. From the bottom of my heart, I pray that people will read this book and develop a better relationship with you, Father, and that you will fill each and every one of them with your joy, love, peace. That whoever reads this will be overtaken by your power, will be so free that they desire nothing more than to serve you, Heavenly Father. I plead the blood of Jesus over each and every person who reads this and ask for their guardian angels to watch over them through this day. I love you so much, Father, and ask for these things in Jesus' name. Amen.

Chapter Two
Amendment 1

Love

Love is such an important topic, yet it is so immense that people find it intimidating and stay away from dissecting this amazing concept. Love is what life is about. It can change people, communities, societies, and even the world. Before we get too far into this topic, I want you to take a few seconds and start thinking of the most important people in your life. Now, in the space below, I want you to write the names of the people in your life who mean the most to you (people you have an actual relationship with).

The people who mean the most to me are:

____

____

____

____

____

____

Now that you've identified those people you care about the most, I have an assignment for you. I urge you to do this for several reasons because: one, it is simple, and two, I promise you it will change your life, or rather enhance your life. When you are on your deathbed years down the road (I have talked to people who have told me this on their deathbeds), and someone asks, "What do you wish you'd done more, or what are your regrets?" don't let it be said that it's not spending enough time with the people who mean the most to you. So your first task is this: start spending more time with the people on your list. Go out of your way to plan time together, to see them and talk to them. Next (this part is hard for many people, but it is a must if you want change in your life), let the people on the list know how much they mean to you. I will give you two options. You can tell them verbally. (Saying, "They know how I feel; I don't need to tell them," does not count. People need to hear that they are loved.) Or you can write (not text). Write them a letter telling them how much you love them, how much they mean to you, how important they are to you. Do this and I promise that not only will they be set free from things and feel loved (everyone wants and needs to feel loved), but you will also feel a thousand pounds lighter. Chains will start to be broken. You will start to smile again. This is another step closer to freedom. 1 John 4:8 says, "Whoever does not love does not know God, because God is love."

Now that we've talked about freedom, let us take that a step further and ask this question: What does "freedom" mean?

I want you to write your understanding of freedom:

____

____

____.

Quotes about Freedom

"Freedom is never voluntarily given by the oppressor; it must be demanded by the oppressed." — Martin Luther King Jr.

"To a soldier, freedom is a responsibility. To a prisoner ... freedom is being able to choose how they spend their time, what they eat, and how they live their life. Perhaps the simplest definition would be: to have the ability to do whatever one wants, wishes, or chooses. But I think that begs the question, what is driving those desires, wishes, choices? Consider then that no man is really free. He or she is a slave to what drives their actions and thoughts. Whether to good or to evil, to God or to Satan. Unfortunately, ever since mankind first ate from the tree of the knowledge of good and evil, we are all subconsciously driven by what we interpret to be good or evil. Herein lies the problem: there are no absolutes in this approach. All are 'free' to choose to conduct themselves in a manner they think appropriate." — Aaron Harris

History of Fighting for Freedom

Freedom Clause is based on different amendments with one simple concept. Before going over the other amendments in the book, you need to embrace and accept the main concept, because without the main concept, the other amendments will not work. The only true way to become free in this world is through love. Lack of love enslaves, shackles, and tortures people. When I mention love, most people think of sex or fairy tales with happy endings. We do not really think of love as it actually is and what it is capable of. First, love is a choice. Like anything else, it comes down to what we choose to do.

God wants to bring you to a place of freedom. In order to get there, we have to realize what love is. The world defines "love" as an emotion of strong affection and personal attachment. Love is compassion and kindness. People say there are two different types of love. You can love objects, food, goals—if you are deeply committed to them—and so on. Then there's love of people (you can include yourself). This is the one that gives us so much trouble in life, the one that causes pain, happiness, joy, and wars. This is the one we all struggle with because we often base this love on a feeling. The Bible talks about four different kinds of love: *phileo*, brotherly love between friends; *eros*, romantic or basically love for the opposite sex; *storge*, a love that you have for a family member; and *agape*, God's love for us—the ultimate love, the ultimate sacrifice.

Think about this next sentence: "God so loved the world that he gave his only son." I want you to think of that and what it really means to you. I like how it reads in the amplified version, "For God so greatly loved and dearly prized the world that He (even) gave up His only begotten (unique) Son." Meditate on that kind of love and write down what you think of it, how it applies in your life, and how you demonstrate it in your day-to-day activities.

For God so greatly loved: This type of love means ___ to me. I show this type of love by ___.

____

____

____

____

This Type of Love Is the Never-Changing Love of God

After years of working with hurting people—working in schools, with troubled youth in detention centers, with adults in rehab, with adults in prison, with middle school children who act out worse than the men in prison—I've learned a few things. One day I sat down and began to pray and ask God to shine light on the commonalities between all the places and people I have spent the better part of my life. Then I started to think of my past—when I was one of these kids—and I started to draw connections. I kept praying, asking for revelation on how to deal with this number of people whom God seemed to continually put in my path. There was a particular middle school where some of the worst behaved youth I ever worked with attended. The school kept putting more rules in the program I was working for, and the result was this: the behavior got worse. I truly have never seen a behavior like this in my entire life. This place was out of control. To say it was chaos would be giving the school too much credit, because I can handle chaos. This school was so bad that the human race has not made a word for it yet. I looked at it as a battlefield. Knowing that the adults were supposed to be preparing these young people to be "our future" was scary. The system wasn't working, and they needed help.

I will give you a brief story, so you can get an idea of what I am talking about. On my first week in the school, there were four fights. Police was called, and a child was taken out on a stretcher. If that was all, that would still be a lot. But it wasn't. One of the teachers brought in her twenty-four-year-old daughter and had her fight one of the eighth grade girls who had been picking on that teacher. The grand finale of my first week happened on a Saturday. I woke up to the morning news where it was reported that the school was broken into by four students (who got caught) stealing the computers out of the computer lab. Things just got worse from there. During my second week, I was just walking in the hall when a seventh grader no taller than the middle of my chest decided to start yelling at me and trying to get me to punch him. This incident was followed by a marijuana bust of an eighth grader who had weed in his locker, which his dad had him bring to the school to sell. This was the environment I was dealing with when I asked God to show me the common factors. What was missing from each group? What did they have in common? What did they need in order to change? How could I reach them? What would have a lasting effect? What changed me? *His answer?* Love. Love gives hope. And hope gives people desires and a sense of self-worth.

So the first amendment in this book is love. Love always pays a price. If we can understand this type of love, our lives will be changed forever. I'd like to share with you a part of a sermon I wrote, which will highlight the *amendment of love.* Before I do that, I want to tell you about two of the main concepts. One is that rules, regulations, or laws cannot change the condition of the human soul; only love can. The other is that love is a SACRIFICIAL action! Love always cost something; it is expensive. When you learn to love, benefits take place in another person's life. Love is not shellfish; it is ment to be shared. It gives and it does not take. Love is both an action and a choice. I want you to mediate on those two concepts for a second and write down in the space below what they mean to you or what is being said by the Holy Spirit to you right now as you read them.

1) **Rules, regulations, and laws cannot change the condition of the human soul. Only love can.**
   a. ____
      ____
      ____
      ____
   b. **How WILL you implement this concept into your life?**
      i. ____
         ____
         ____
         ____

2) **Love is a SACRIFICIAL action!" Love always cost something; it is expensive. When you learn to love, benefits take place to another person's life. Love is for someone else. It gives and it does not take. Love is both an action and a choice.**

a. ____

____

____

____

b. **How will I implement this concept in my life to change my relationships and people I do not even know?**

i. ____

____

____

____

____

Love worth Fighting For

"If you love someone, let them go. If they come back to you, then they are yours!" I grew up hearing this saying, and I loved it. I never knew what it meant, but I loved it. Now that I understand love, it makes sense and I love it even more. True love is putting other people's needs, desires, and wants ahead of your own. It is a sacrifice of oneself for another person. This goes against all of our instincts as humans, but it is what God called us to do and how he called us to love. Let's take that one step further because it is easy to love people we naturally care about, like our wives, husbands, kids, and so on. But what will truly change the world is when we do this for people we do not know, such as those we encounter at the local grocery store, the gas station, or restaurant. This is when we start showing the love of Jesus.

Love is completely selfless. This is a hard concept to understand, especially in this generation. Sure, we like to help people, have friends, or give a hand now and again, but how many of us truly put our interests aside for someone else? I bet that if you have, it hasn't been consistent. Perhaps you've tried it once or twice, but not always. It's not how we live our life day in and day out. Now this is what love is— God so loved the world that he GAVE his only son (John 3:16). He didn't want to see Jesus being tortured and murdered, but His love for us made Him give up His only Son to die for us, so we could be saved. He gave something up in order to receive sorrow, hurt, pain, loss, and grief. He did this so we could receive freedom, happiness, joy, and deliverance. God has proven that love is completely selfless.

I challenge you to think right now. Have you ever really loved anyone the way God truly wants us to love?

I Remember When I Loved Someone like This

First, I'll tell you that I talk about her throughout this book. I will not get into the details now, but I think this story helps explain that type of love as close as possible or as close as we will ever see on earth. I loved my mom so much. She was at the prime of her life. She was young, in her forties. But she was facing the end of her life. She's in such gut-wrenching pain without relief from cancer.

I mean if you've ever experienced this horrible disease, then you know what I am talking about. You reach a point where pain meds can't even come close to touching the pain. You are stuck there helpless. There's nothing you can do as the person you love the most in the world is screaming in pain, begging to die, asking what she did to deserve this pain, and why won't it stop. You watch the person you love plead God for a second chance, beg for healing. You watch a human life suffer to the extent that she looks at you behind closed doors at one in the morning and starts begging you to kill her, to put a pillow over her head and end her pain. Picture the person you love the most in this world suffering, and you are helpless. This puts anger inside of you deep down, burying itself, layer upon layer, inside your stomach. After years of believing for a chance to be healed, there came a point where she wanted to go to heaven, and the pastor watching over her told us we need to release her. I would watch her suffer and still not let her go. Inside,

I was holding on. She was my mom with or without pain. I wanted her here. This went on for months. Doctors said she wouldn't make it past the night, and yet months passed. Why did she remain? Because my love was so strong I could not let her go. I would tell her, "I need you. Please do not leave me. I loved you so much." So one day I saw how she could not move, go to the bathroom, eat, or talk, and I just painfully looked at her. Then I did the most selfless thing I could do. I whispered to her, "Mom, it is OK. You can go home to God. I love you. I will be fine. Go home." Later that day she passed away. Every single fiber in my being wanted my mom to stay around, but I loved her so much that I knew what was best for her. And I needed to put her needs ahead of my own.

As I pictured how much pain, frustration, and hurt that incident brought, I imaged God going through the same type of thing. That experience is as close as I can come to understanding this: Picture God, the master of the universe, watching His Son get tortured, torn apart, spit on, made fun of. His Son cried out for help in pain on the cross. God sat by; He let His Son go through that for us. That is how much love He has for us.

Love is when you stop thinking of yourself and start thinking of other people.

1) **Love values the other person:**
   - o Not a feeling
   - o Not lust
   - o Gratification
   - o VALUE
     - ▪ Love is an active interest in the well-being of another person.
     - ▪ Love acts for the benefit of others.

Example:

God loved us NOT because we had something to offer him, but because he had something to offer us.

2) **Love is vulnerable to others:**
   - o Love opens up its life to one another.
     - James 5:16

3) **Love entails a cost:**
   - o Jesus gave his blood. It cost his life.
     - Love makes a statement and leaves a legacy.
     - It performs acts that steal the heart and forever changes the soul.

With this being said, I challenge you to stop thinking of your own problems all the time—your health, job situation, life, bills—get proactive and start to walk in love, so much so that you are thinking of other people's problems. Start to pray for other people's problems. If we do this, the devil will be like, "What is going on? You have your own problems. Why are you praying for them?" All you have to say is, "Devil, shut up." When you pray for others, it puts your faith working for others. And when this happens, it opens the doors wide open for God to flood your life with blessings. Everything Jesus did, he did by faith working in love. It only takes one person walking in the love of God to feel His presence that will change whatever place he or she is in. Pain, helplessness, defeat, or addiction usually all comes from lack of love. If you break it down, lack of self-love or love from family will produce these things in your life. The love of God is the only thing that can break these chains and rip out the root from within you and set you free. Everything comes from love. Love is a choice, not a feeling. Feelings come and go, but true love is a decision to stay with it forever.

Scriptures

John 3:16

For God so loved the world, that he gave his only Son, that whoever believes in him should not perish but have eternal life.

Romans 5:8

But God shows his love for us in that while we were still sinners, Christ died for us.

Romans 8:37–39

No, in all these things we are more than conquerors through him who loved us. For I am sure that neither death nor life, nor angels nor rulers, nor things present nor things to come, nor powers, nor height nor depth, nor anything else in all creation, will be able to separate us from the love of God in Christ Jesus our Lord.

Galatians 2:20

I have been crucified with Christ. It is no longer I who live, but Christ who lives in me. And the life I now live in the flesh I live by faith in the Son of God, who loved me and gave himself for me.

1 John 3:1

See what kind of love the Father has given to us, that we should be called children of God; and so we are. The reason why the world does not know us is that it did not know him.

Romans 13:8

Owe no one anything, except to love each other, for the one who loves another has fulfilled the law.

Galatians 5:13

For you were called to freedom, brothers. Only do not use your freedom as an opportunity for the flesh, but through love serve one another.

Ephesians 4:2

With all humility and gentleness, with patience, bearing with one another in love.

1 Peter 1:22

Having purified your souls by your obedience to the truth for a sincere brotherly love, love one another earnestly from a pure heart.

1 John 4:7

Beloved, let us love one another, for love is from God, and whoever loves has been born of God and knows God.

Matthew 5:43–48

You have heard that it was said, "You shall love your neighbor and hate your enemy." But I say to you, Love your enemies and pray for those who persecute you, so that you may be sons of your Father who is in heaven. For he makes his sun rise on the evil and on the good, and sends rain on the just and on the unjust. For if you love those who love you, what reward do you have? Do not even the tax collectors do the same? And if you greet only your brothers, what more are you doing than others? Do not even the Gentiles do the same? You therefore must be perfect, as your heavenly Father is perfect.

Matthew 6:24–25

No one can serve two masters, for either he will hate the one and love the other, or he will be devoted to the one and despise the other. You cannot serve God and money. "Therefore I tell you, do not be anxious about your life, what you will eat or what you will drink, nor about your body, what you will put on. Is not life more than food, and the body more than clothing?

Mark 12:28–30

And one of the scribes came up and heard them disputing with one another, and seeing that he answered them well, asked him, "Which commandment is the most important of all?" Jesus answered, "The most important is, 'Hear, O Israel: The Lord our God, the Lord is one. And you shall love the Lord your God with all your heart and with all your soul and with all your mind and with all your strength."

John 14:21–24

Whoever has my commandments and keeps them, it is he who loves me. And he who loves me will be loved by my Father, and I will love him and manifest myself to him. Judas (not Iscariot) said to him, "Lord, how is it that you will manifest yourself to us, and not to the world?" Jesus answered him, "If anyone loves me, he will keep my word, and my Father will love him, and we will come to him and make our home with him. Whoever does not love me does not keep my words. And the word that you hear is not mine but the Father's who sent me."

John 15:9–17

As the Father has loved me, so have I loved you. Abide in my love. If you keep my commandments, you will abide in my love, just as I have kept my Father's commandments and abide in his love. These things I have spoken to you, that my joy may be in you, and that your joy may be full. "This is my commandment, that you love one another as I have loved you. Greater love has no one than this, that someone lay down his life for his friends. You are my friends if you do what I command you. No longer do I call you servants, for the servant does not know what his master is doing; but I have called you friends, for all that I have heard from my Father I have made known to you. You did not choose me, but I chose you and appointed you that you should go and bear fruit and that your fruit should abide, so that whatever you ask the Father in my name, he may give it to you. These things I command you, so that you will love one another."

Chapter Three
Amendment 2

Write a Confession to God

This amendment is the structure of freedom clause to me. This is the most important thing in my life that brought me absolute change. All these amendments will bring you freedom, but this one forms the base, the root; it's the structure for all the rest. At least for me, it is. This is the first step I took that made me feel alive, full of joy, and free for the first time in my life. After this one step, the rest of the amendments will get so much easier for you. If you do what this chapter tells you to do, then I believe 100 percent that the Holy Spirit will minister to you, and you will feel freedom for the first time in your life or for the first time in many years. This is what I want you to do: write down all the things you are expecting God to free you from, things you've been praying for years to be freed from. Example: worry, mental pain, failure, hopelessness, anger, hate, jealously, suicide, drugs, and so forth—whatever you are enslaved to.

Things that have been keeping me enslaved:

Now I want you to copy this next sentence on the lines provided below. *I believe that today, after I finish this chapter by the power of the Holy Spirit, God will set me free from every shackle, every chain, every grip that the enemy has on me. I believe that from this day on, I will be truly set free. God, give me freedom. Thank you, Father. Amen.*

I remember the second time I tried to kill myself. I had so much pain inside of me, so much hurt, so much hopelessness, and I had no feelings of love—just defeat. I was a slave to these feelings, and no matter what I did, I could not find freedom. I cried out to God, "Please, just take this pain away and show me freedom from all this hurt." When he did not answer, I thought I would help him out and take my own way out of this game called life. I figured that if I cashed out, I would finally be pain free, hurt free; I would be truly set free.

Freedom to me was something different than what freedom may mean to you. So I want you to write down what is freedom to you? What does your freedom look like? What is your personal definition of freedom?

What freedom used to mean to me was to make it through a day without wanting to die. It meant to be able to sit and think without worrying about all the pains in my life. It meant taking this massive self-eating pain I had inside my stomach that would slowly work through my bloodstream, tearing up everything it came across with little razors of poison, to finally go away for the first time. It meant that I would be able to smile for the first time in years and laugh. I spent years feeling dead inside. I do not say that as a matter of speech; I actually felt dead. I had no emotions, just pain that would cause me to react in anger. Joy was impossible for me. Happiness was a myth made up by modern movie production agencies. So to me, freedom was a mental and emotional process. There had been times in my life when my physical freedom was in jeopardy, but that to me was nothing compared to my mental and emotional freedom. If I had to sum it up in a sentence, freedom to me was the wish to feel joy again, to hope. It is the wish to want to live life again, to no longer be locked down, caged with rage in this world, and to be a slave to hopelessness. Freedom is to have self-love again, to feel God's love again, and to accept it, believe in it, focus on it. So that is why I personally think freedom is love. When someone loves you or you love him or her, you are bringing glory to them. When you bring glory to yourself, something is wrong. Love is out of balance, and you start to lose your freedom by becoming self-absorbed with pride. We must realize and focus on the fact that God wants us in a place of freedom. We just have to allow that freedom into our lives. That freedom will change you.

Think about it. Things in life can take away our freedom. As I mentioned earlier, pain, helplessness, defeat, and/or addiction usually come from lack of love someplace—lack of love from family or self. Most youth that do drugs or have tried drugs tell me—and this shocked me–that they did it not because they were curious. That is what the world wants us to think. It's what we hear in schools. It's what we've been telling ourselves for centuries—that kids do drugs because they are curious or because of peer pressures. *(Side note: I did find peer pressure to be a contributor as to why youth do drugs, but 80 percent of the youth have or do drugs because of family pressures—to escape pressure, to run away from problems, and/or to subdue stress. These were seventh through twelfth graders in different circumstances and settings. Then I found that these kids were lacking hope and love at home. They felt destined for a future of despair and hurt. There is nothing more challenging and rewarding than giving hope to a young student who has no hope. They need to experience love. And to offer true freedom to someone is to give them love. Jesus gave us true freedom. He delivered us from all sufferings in life and gives us hope. Jesus is love. Jesus is freedom. Everything comes from love. Love is a choice,* not a feeling. *Applying logic on those last two statements, it could be concluded that freedom is a choice. This is why people in prison or slavery can still choose to experience freedom.)*

The problem I got was that I knew about Jesus' love. I'd heard about it, read about it, believed in it, but I did not *feel* it. I figured that maybe I'd done so much wrong in life that I was unable to feel his love, so therefore I would never experience freedom. Eventually, I became "OK" with this thought. I figured everyone else in the church world is experiencing true freedom. They feel love and joy. I learned to simply be happy for them. I remember telling God in a prayer after begging to feel happiness, love, and hope, "Father, I am not going to leave you ever. I am in this to the end, so I will suck up this feeling of pain, defeat, and hopelessness, and just fake that I am happy." I truly believed with all my heart that this was going to be "it" for the rest of my life—I was going to be dead inside with pain, anger, and hopelessness while watching everyone around me happy and filled with joy and love. The sad part was that after I accepted I would never feel these things, I began to tell myself that I didn't deserve them. I'd been through so much and done so much that I deserved to feel miserable at all times. So I accepted following God while still feeling dead and miserable inside. *(Quick side note: Years later—and I thank God that I did this—I learned that serving God has nothing to do with feelings. We are to serve God no matter what we are feeling that day. That being said, God does want us to be happy, have hope, love, and joy, so I spent a year crying out to God, "Why will you not allow me to feel these things in my life? What must I do to feel anything positive inside? I just want to feel hope again.")* I do not care what anyone else says. When you lose hope in life, you lose life itself. Nothing matters anymore. "Hope deferred makes the heart sick" (Proverbs 13:12). The feeling of hope is so strong that without it, life is a scary place because you just do not care about anything—not life, not death. You are just here, existing. At one point, I remember a situation that had gone horribly wrong, which ended with someone putting a gun to my head. Because I didn't care, I just looked at him without feeling angry or even scared, and I simply said, "Do me a favor, please. If not, get that gun away from my head and walk away before I kill you." People thought I was tough, hard, a gangster, but that was not the case. I was just hopeless; I did not care about anything. I would shake at night and wake up crying, yelling, or worse, completely emotionless.

I would go to church, raise my hands, praise God, and sing, yet inside still I felt nothing. I would walk through the church, shake hands, and hug people. I even started volunteering with youth to talk with them about the love of God. But inside I was empty.

I finally had a break down. I had my **Ziklag moment**. A Ziklag moment is that time in my life when I had nobody to turn to; everyone was gone. I was hurting and out of options, so I yelled to God, "It is you and me God. You need to prove yourself real to me, because I cannot go on." Perhaps you're at your Ziklag point.

Let's look at 1 Samuel chapter 30. Here we'll find David in Ziklag. Ziklag was a Philistine town where David and his men took refuge. Once, when David and his army were away, the Amalekites attacked and ravaged Ziklag. They kidnaped all the women and children—wives, daughters, sons. When David and his army returned, he saw the disaster; everything was destroyed, burnt to the ground. All the families including his were missing. Men, warriors, and soldiers turned into fathers, sons, and brothers. They stood in the middle of the smoke and cried until they could not physically cry anymore. This had to be the worst day of David's life. David could have given up, taken over by pain. But nobody has ever fulfilled their purpose by giving up. Just when you think things could not get any worse, they got worse. David's own men, the men he loved, whom he lead for years in and out of battle turned their backs on him and started talking about stoning him. This was David's breaking point. What to do? Do you retreat? Quit? Turn and give in to your dark feelings? Think about how alone David must have felt. How betrayed he felt. He had no friends; his family was gone. There was nothing but him and his thoughts of defeat and pain. He was forced to turn to God and God alone; nobody else. He had nobody to talk to in his moment of despair; he had nobody to text, call, or e-mail. David encouraged and strengthened himself in his Lord, his God.

There I was in my car one evening in June when I faced my Ziklag moment. I was upset already because the girl I was seeing would not answer any of my calls or texts. For some reason, this particular time, I just started to get lost in my own mind. I started to think of the death of my mom, my grandmother, and my aunt. I thought of how my dad left me at a young age, how I had been homeless, and how I'd almost gone to prison for fifteen years. Negative thoughts raced through my mind, reminding me of how I lost everything I ever owned, how every girlfriend I ever had either left me or cheated on me. I fixated on how the girl I had been talking to for nearly two years was not returning my calls or my texts. And to make matters worse, she was leaving, relocating for good the next day. I pulled over and sat in a parking lot with all these thoughts eating at me, making fun of me, torturing me. I had nothing; I had no place to live. I was living with a friend on the couch. I had nobody in my life. I started to think death would be much easier; I just wanted to die to stop the pain. Nothing else would change. Death was my only option. And at that moment, everything around me became black. I literally could not see, and I was crying out loud like a kid cries when he needs milk to survive. I felt as though something was inside my intestines trying to eat its way out of my body. I started to get flashes of vision, dark to red. Then I could see the street in front of me. Then it was back to black, red, and then straight in front of me. The pain was fighting for release. I screamed, "Lord, if you do not take this pain away, I will kill someone or myself!" I thought that if I killed someone, I could use that to let the pain out of me, make that person feel what I was feeling and that in so doing, I would feel relief.

I started to panic. The desire was so real, so intense, that it seemed inevitable. I started to call and text everyone of my friends—nobody answered. This has never happened to me. I texted my friends, "I'm going crazy. I want to end it right now. Someone please help me." Nobody answered. I texted my brother just to see what he was doing. Nobody answered. I texted other people and left one friend a message: "I am going to kill myself. Please, I just need to talk to you." Nobody answered. It was like God wanted to deal with just me in our Ziklag moment. I am not proud of the next part, but it is part of my story, so I am going to tell it. I finally got out of my car and started to walk the streets, looking for someone to fight or kill. I grabbed my brass knuckles and some mace and started to walk. My thoughts truly said to me, *If you hurt someone else bad enough, this would let all that pain out of your body. Just give it to someone else.* I saw no one, not one single person. Eventually, I calmed down enough and went back to my car, then I drove to the house I was staying. I grabbed a six-pack of Twisted Tea, walked upstairs, and said to God, "If you aren't going to help me, then I will help you. Here's your chance. Take me tonight. Please. I will make it easy for you." I took a few sleeping pills, a Xanax bar, and some hydrocodone. I slammed that six packs of tea and mixed it with some whisky. I gave God my ultimatum:

either kill me now tonight or heal all this pain inside me. I cannot go on this way. I fell into a deep sleep.

The next day, I woke up around one in the afternoon with a headache—five hours late for work. But I woke up. How did I wake up? To this day, there is no other answer other than a miracle from God, because the second I woke up, I felt God telling me, "It is not your time yet. You are not done with what I called you to do."

I searched deep down inside to see what I felt, and it was all still there. I remember this moment well. I said to God, "Please, I just need this pain to go away. I tried to kill myself, but you would not let me. So tell me how I can be set free."

I felt the Spirit talk to me, and it said, "You are almost there. You've partially given up your control, and you now realize that *you* cannot fix anything. You have to let me take complete control of your life, then you will be free."

I made a promise to him right there in my bed. I said, "Father, I should have died; therefore I am dead. This is now your body and your life. Whatever you want me to do, I will do. Whatever door you open, I will go through. Father, use me for whatever you want me; I am all yours."

Then once again I heard this voice inside, plain as day. It told me that in order to be free, I needed to go someplace where I wouldn't be disturbed, and write my confession, all my sins, my fears, and disappointments. I immediately grabbed my laptop and drove to the nearest coffee shop, got some coffee, and began to type. As I typed, I felt varied emotions. I wrote and I cried. A few hours later, it was completed. I then felt 65 percent better; I was amazed. It felt like I could breathe for the first time. I told the Father thank you, but I asked him to give me complete freedom. I wanted the full 100 percent. I wanted to feel love and hope again. Before I could finish my sentence, I heard a voice inside say, "Send it to someone."

I said, "No. Not a chance."

Again, I heard the voice. "Send it to someone."

Again I said, "No."

There were things in this confession that had the power to destroy me. The voice said, "Expose yourself and trust me. Be completely free."

So without thinking, I wrote an e-mail to my sister-in-law and attached my letter. Instantly, I felt 100 percent free. Love, joy, and hope began to swell on the inside. I began to laugh out loud and smile from ear to ear. It was like God miraculously lifted all my sorrow, pain, and hurt and replaced them with His love and hope. It felt so good. I even sent it to two more people before I left the coffeehouse—just because. It was amazing. To this day, of all the miracles I've witnessed in my life, the coffeehouse experience is my favorite.

This is a basic biblical principle. I know that some people are concerned about the confession part. I used to be one of those people. I felt I only needed to confess to God, but there is something so powerful about bringing your sins out of the dark and into the light before others. Let's look at James 5:16. It reads, "Confess to one another therefore your faults (your skips, your false steps, your offenses, your sins) and pray [also] for one another, that you may be healed and restored (to a spiritual tone of mind and heart). The earnest (heartfelt, continued) prayer of righteous man makes tremendous power available [dynamic in its working]."

I am going to break down the word "confess" from this verse. The word "confess" in this scripture means *exomologeo*—to confess, to profess, to acknowledge openly and joyfully. It is used the same as the word "confess" in Matthew 3:6: "and they were baptized by him in the river Jordan, confessing their sins."

So what aids us in healing hurt, pain, sickness, defeat, death, or suicidal thoughts? What sets us free? What breaks our chains and builds us back? Confession does. The word of God says that confessing our faults to one another aids in our healing and restoration. Think about life in general. When we hide things, it eats at us, distracts us, and starts to take over our feelings.

Depending upon how big the "elephant in the room" is, it can take enormous energy to try to hide it from our family and friends. But when we take those things or that thing that we are hiding and tell someone else about it, well then, we receive a release—a sense of freedom from what has been troubling us. We no longer have to carry that burden alone. *(An important side note is this: use wisdom when you decide it's time to write and share your confession with someone. Pray about it and only share it with someone God highlights to you whom you know has been proven to be trustworthy and nonjudgmental. Do not share it with your neighbor Miss Becky, who is known as the neighborhood gossip queen, the one who can tell you the last time your aunts, uncles, sisters, and nephews visited your house and what they were wearing. If you decide to tell your confession to this person, and she shared your secret to the entire state of New York within six hours, do not be surprised or blame this process for your newly found lack of privacy. This is why I am saying use wisdom and pray for God to show you whom to give the letter to.)* My last point is this: we do not always have to confess all our faults to someone. However, that being said, there are times in life when it can be very helpful. I believe this is the point and time in your life to confess. That is why the Spirit led you to read this book—this is the time. Confess, bring things to light, and watch the joy shower you.

This is the most important step in the book, so make sure you do this step. I implore you to trust me better yet trust God. It will be worth it, and you will be free. There is no darkness in light. To encourage you to embrace your own journey towards the light, towards freedom, I am sharing my confession with you now. It is the same letter I sent to my sister-in-law after my failed suicide attempt. The letter I was afraid to send, which then ultimately set me free, I now share with you. Here is my confession

(Side note: To help you, here are the steps I took: I prayed then started to write about emotions—my pains, my frustrations, my deepest fears—and from there, just kept writing. Write about

your sins that you never told anyone. Get everything from deep inside you out. Keep writing until you feel like a thousand pounds has been lifted from your chest. If someone has hurt you—a parent, wife, husband, friend—write a letter telling them how they hurt you, what they did, and forgive them.)

Before you read this, I must warn you that when I free write out of emotion, my ADHD kicks in and my brain goes in a million different directions at once. And at times, I like to rhyme when I free write. While writing this book, I had to control all those urges. But this confession was a free emotional writing exercise, and you will be reading the uncut rhyming and eight-different-direction confession. I have taken out a few things for self-protection and privacy, but 95 percent of it is the original content.

Confession to God

I feel as though I have to write. I feel as though God has been telling me for years to get back to writing. I kept putting it off. I have a burning feeling inside that will not leave; I have to get it out. I have felt this way for years, but I don't know how much fight I have left in me. I have done so much wrong. I've been locked down in chains, trapped in a mental prison, trapped in hell filled with pain and rage. It has been hard to see straight, to focus; my mind has been a high-speed war zone going thousands of different ways a second. I have known God. I have gone to church. I praise him. But I still was alone in this battle. I thought, "I can do this." I can take it on myself. I forgot what it was like to be happy; I forgot what it was like to be sane. Mental breakdowns started to become nightly things. Suicidal thoughts, pills to sleep, hatred and anger were growing by each breath. But still I would go to church with a smile and a cross on my chest. I tell everyone it is fine. I crack a joke to keep people out of my mind. They could see the good in me; I have a heart for people like no other. I feel pain when they feel pain, I love when they love. I get so connected to people's souls it sometimes becomes unsafe—because I can love someone like God loves them. And then when they hurt me, it destroys me. People do not understand. Then the flesh takes over. People don't see the anger, the pain that builds up from a life of hell. Thoughts of hurting, destroying someone and his entire family haunt me. I fight it, but it tries to come out. I bury it but it seeps out. I am that type of guy whom they could say, "I never thought he would do that; he was so well liked and funny." I keep finding myself lost in the wilderness, and somehow I make it out. Now, once again, I find myself lost and feel there is more to come. I am alone, but I am holding onto God because I do not think it is time for me to come home.

The world has beaten me time and time again. Since birth, I have been surrounded by pain and defeat. I always felt God even when I didn't know him. He has given me so many chances on my way. He wants me to change, and I do for a short time, but I bounce right back. I haven't lived a long life, but I have been through a thousand people's worst nights. I've been beaten. I've been alone. I've been emotionally scarred and abandoned in my own home; that was all before the age of twelve. As a young teen, I had girls stealing for me. I've talked friends into drinking, smoking weed. I've lead people down the wrong path, sometimes just to get a laugh. I've been in fights, hurt people—kicked them when they were down ... so much anger, it felt so good to put other people's life in danger.

I've been rich, I've been poor. I thought poor was bad, but then later in life, I found myself homeless, jobless, moneyless. I have seen death, so much death. I lost almost my entire family, and I watched them all go, praying to God to let them stay as I watched my mom suffer each day. I have sold drugs, done drugs. I sold small amounts as a teen, thought I was a "bad" man. That little one day turned into a lot that then turned into more and more power. I have always been popular, well liked. But this was a different feeling. I had what people could not get; people didn't know how I got it. I had connections. I had people who would kill for me, and it's not like what your friends say to you, I mean real suit-and-tie-wearing people who owned business, driving Escalades, and would sit you down in an office and say, "Give me a name and it is taken care of." I have seen temptation, I've helped people sin. I talked to God and would say to myself, "I am doing what I am doing, and He understands. After all, God, you took my mom, left me all alone. Nobody cares about me, and I have to do what I have to do to survive. Because if I don't, nobody else will.

I have been close to death more than once. Sickness has haunted me for months. I have beaten people, and it felt great. All that anger just leaving as I would punch, kick, and hate. I have had guns pulled on me and laughed. I was in so much pain I truly didn't fear death. People knew me as crazy, insane. I would never back down; I've walked into a crowd of people who want to fight. All alone I stood my ground.

I have degrees, education. Coworkers see me as happy-go-lucky. No idea about what I have done or who I have become. I have had good jobs. I ran a facility. Criminal justice is my degree, and my teachers were in love with me. I worked with youth; I have guided and counseled. I have trained professionals; I have taught classes. I have robbed, stolen money, as I would pray, "Dear God, forgive me. But look at what that world has done to me." People had no idea I was selling drugs, hanging out with real gangsters and thugs.

I prayed to die. I prayed, "Forgive me, Father, it's time to change. Take away this rage. That change only lasted a few days."

I've had chest pains. On the way to the hospital, I prayed, "Heal me, Father, and I'll change." A pastor who is like my dad prayed healing for me. My best friend, my brother miles and miles away, somehow knew what was going on that day and broke down without a call from anyone. He put his face down in the dirt and prayed. They found nothing; the pain went away. God healed me once again. I sang his name. That time I changed for a month or so.

I've been in love. I've been hurt. Loved again that lead to worse hurt. I just recently tried to hold on to my last girlfriend, and she hurt me even worse than any of the others have before. I have seen a lot, and I keep seeing more. Pain keeps forcing itself through my front door.

My aunt got sick, the last mom-like figure in my life. She passed away. Now I am ready to change, still have rage, still have pain.

Now I have symptoms again, thinking the worse. I get prayed for. Doctors can't find anything. God heals again. I know I have to truly change this time, or he will just take my life and write "the end." I keep staying clean, but life catches up. My phone was tapped. "Wow," how life keeps catching up. I've been fired. God, I am so tired. As I am being questioned, I hear you could get fifteen years.

Months pass, I try to pray. I keep all this pain inside. Anger eats at me. Death haunts me. I can't find peace. I lose my home, not much family left. No place to go. I feel so depressed. God puts a friend in my life that I knew of back in high school. Met him at church. Gives me a place to live. Still have no money; in debt beyond belief. But I have a place to lay my head at night.

I keep pressing on. I keep praying. I get closer and closer to God. I get more temptations, but I stay focused. A year passes; I'm still doing well. People keep tracking me down; temptations kept growing. At night, I'm still haunted by anger, pain, and thoughts. I miss my mom, my aunt, my family. I just don't know how much longer I can go on. Things keep beating me down. No charges are brought up against me; nobody involved can figure out how. It's like they forgot all about me, and all the pictures and wiretaps seemed to just disappear. It was like God himself surrounded me and said, "You are not touching my son. He is mine. I will deal with him for what he has done, but you are not touching my son."

God creates a job for me. When I say "creates a job," he took my passion and knowledge on a topic and made a job. It was the first one ever offered in New York. It was a created position. I applied scared because every other job I'd applied for resulted in reference calls to my old job, which in return would say, "Call the federal prison and they will tell you about his work history." I applied, got interviewed, and got the job.

Still going to church. Still pressing on. But I still feel this pain, this anger, this hatred. I think I am just bad inside. I pray and I try and try to change, but this rage keeps building up each day. I smile. I laugh. But at night, all alone I cry and ask God, "Why am I alone without anyone to hold?" I keep going to church. I keep trying. There is no way I will go back to my old ways, and that I can put in writing.

More pain now, more anger, more rage, but whatever I am used to pain. I am thinking, "God, I tried to change. Did I fail you? Please just take away this pain. I've been walking for you this last year. I know you love me. I just want to please you." Inside, I feel convicted. He told me to look around me and push certain people away. "I've been doing so good, God, but look at all my pain. My family suffered and died. We cried for your name. My brother has been going through fire for years now, and he walks with you every day. My sister-in-law is having chest pains; doctor visits again. What is up with all this rain? She has faith, not scared. She is going through her storm with strength and still finds time to help me. I hear you telling me there are still some things that must change."

Everyone keeps leaving out of my life—girls, friends. Everyone seems to always leave me. This pain, this rage, is worse than ever before. I cannot move, can't think. How can people be so heartless? I want to die. I want to kill. So angry that I taste blood in my lungs; I throw up. I shake. I think. My dad up and left me, grandma died, mom died, my aunt died—they all left me. Girls have come and gone; friends have moved on. Then this girl I've been talking to comes along, rips out my soul, takes my emotions out of control, then ups and leaves, not saying a word.

I think of suicide again to end this pain. So much pain, so much worry, so alone. Took pills and liquor to go to bed that night, hoping I won't wake up. I wake up. Maybe God doesn't want me yet.

I am under so much pressure; it hurts to breathe. Pain in my body that haunts me is making it hard to sleep. I can't focus at night, and I still have faith; I still believe. I am on a journey, and I now realize that I just have to let God lead. This past Sunday, Pastor said that sometimes we have to go through trials and cut people out of your life. Oh, God, that is the word that I need. Once again, you are there for me.

As I walked through this life full of pain, my church has been there for me time and time again. My friends and family (that's left) are the best. I love them more than I love myself. I am that type of person who would die for my family or friends. When they hurt, I hurt. God has shown me some things I still need to fix, and I am changing them. I still have anger, so many questions. I haven't been happy in years. But I have this love for God that I cannot explain, and I feel that everything will be OK. I won't give up; it is just hard when you have nothing, not even your own place—no home to run to. You try to walk straight, but to this day, I have so many temptations eating at me, following me.

I feel God has a plan for me. I have no idea what it is. I feel I have so much work to do for him still. I still feel alone and have this rage. I keep asking God to take it away. All I know is I've been through hell and back many times, and I have never stopped believing in God. I have lost so many family members. I have been in so much pain, but I still have faith. I don't look for answers to why things happened; I just trust in God and keep walking. It's all in his hands. That is who I am—a man that fears and loves God till the end. I just hope I have not let him down. I am afraid when I go, he will not say, "Well done, good and faithful servant." That I fear more than anything.

Sincerely,
Colby Sutter

Your Turn

Now I want you to go someplace where nobody will bug you, a place where you can be alone. Then turn off your cell phone and start writing your confession. Take your time, put feeling into it, and write from the heart. Before you start writing, though, pray to God to be set free from whatever you need to be free of. Pray that He shows you every dark part of your life, that He reveals your innermost fears and secrets. Pray that He helps you let them all out. After you are finished writing, I want you to send it to at least one person, telling him or her what it is and what it is about. Send it to someone you can trust, someone you know that will not judge you. Do this and watch how God will set you free. I feel that this part, the sharing, is so important. If you don't have anybody to send it to, then I want you to e-mail it to me, and I will read it and pray over you. Send it to Colby@sevenmiles.org.

Confession: ______________________________________

____

____

____

Scriptures

1 John 1:8

If we confess our sins he is faithful and just and will forgive us our sins and purify us from all unrighteousness.

Acts 3:19–20

Repent, then and turn to God, so that your sins may be wiped out, that times of refreshing may come from the Lord, and that he may send the Christ, who has been appointed for you.

1 John 2:12

My dear children I write this to you so that you will not sin. But if anybody does sin, we have one who speaks to the Father in our defense, Jesus Christ, the righteous one. He is the atoning sacrifice for our sins, and not only for ours but also for the sins of the world.

Afterthought

I have spoken to many youth and to many different churches, schools, and radio stations on the topic of suicide. I feel God has placed this as a number one priority for my heart. That being said, I want to change gears now and spend just a little more time dealing with suicide, which is such a major issue but seldom truly talked about. I feel strongly in my heart that taking this opportunity and pausing from the message of the book will help people understand suicide a little more, and may help someone reading this go through a hard time of grieving over a suicide death or thinking of suicide.

I have read once that in the United States, someone dies every sixteen minutes from suicide, and every one minute, someone attempts suicide. That is sad. Think about that. Life is so hard that every sixteen minutes, we have people taking their own lives to escape. Now this is important. I believe that suicide happens for the most part when pain becomes off balanced, too strong to handle, and we do not have enough coping skills in our life to deal with the built up of the pain. This does not mean you are weak or a loser; you just have more pain than you know how to handle.

Think of it this way. You are in the gym, and you start to pile weight onto your back. You keep adding more and more weight that it becomes heavier and heavier. Now we all have different strength, so we can all handle different amounts of weight. But eventually what will happen? You will fall down. You will collapse from the weight if you keep piling it onto your back. I doesn't matter how bad you want to keep standing or how bad you do not want to collapse. Your will power has nothing to do with it at a certain point. To me this is what pain in our lives can do. If we do not know how to deal with this pain, we will eventually reach a breaking point (suicide). It is not a human defect; it is an imbalance of resources for coping versus pain.

- Some examples of resources for coping.
  - Mom and dad
  - Brother and sister
  - Other family members
  - Friends
  - Activities
    - Exercise
    - Walking
    - Writing
  - Church
    - A real relationship with Jesus

You can overcome suicidal feelings if you find a way to reduce the pain or—if that is impossible—find a way to increase your resources for coping. When I began to teach and educate people on suicide, I noticed that I fit the signs of depression and suicide so perfectly that it was scary.

Signs of Depression and/or Suicidal Tendencies

- You have suffered a loss in a traumatic way.
  - I watched my mom get tortured from the pains of cancer for two years as she begged to die to end her suffering; she even asked me to kill her at times.
- You have suffered losses over a short period of time.

    - o I had three losses in a short period of a time, two within a day; the third came within a year.
- You have chemical addiction or a long length of drug use that can lead to depression.
    - o I started to take pain pills, sleeping pills, and muscle relaxers several times a day.
    - o I started to take pain pills on a daily basis starting in eighth grade.
- You are not grieving properly.
    - o The pills made it impossible for me to grieve the losses I suffered.
- You lost long periods of your life.
    - o I lost years of my life (eight years).
- You turn to other compulsive behaviors.
    - o I started gambling several times a day on a regular basis, and then I became a compulsive gambler.

Breaking Point

A breaking point is an event that causes you to snap or pushes you to that suicidal moment. People think that breaking point is the reason you snapped or tried to commit suicide, but it's the final weight on the shoulders I was talking about earlier that forces you to the brink. For example, a young woman kills herself after her boyfriend breaks up with her. The breakup usually is not the reason; it is just the breaking point, the event that finally pushes the pain so far that death seems to be the only way to stop it. If a person has the right coping skills in their life, the breaking point will hopefully never happen. Of course, there are always exceptions to what I am talking about. I am just generalizing for the sake of argument. When my breaking point happened, I felt like I had no purpose left in life. At this point, I had no job, and I was basically homeless. I had so many bills with no way to pay them. Because of this, all of the valuable possessions I had in storage were taken from me by the storage company. I'd lost another family member to cancer, and I was looking at possible prison time. The girl I was seeing at the time happened to be my breaking point. When she stopped talking to me, everything else just came crashing down all at once. I felt like there was no place to go. I had no family; I felt all alone. All I wanted was someone to hold me and tell me everything would be OK. I felt like I had no purpose left in life, and I needed a purpose. There is no worse pain in this world than feeling all alone. I mean, truly feeling absolutely alone and completely unloved.

When dealing with someone you may think is suicidal, remember a few key things:

1) Be real with them; come from the heart. People can sense when you are pure with your intentions or if you have an agenda. Let the person know that they are not alone and you love them.
    - In my life at this time, I truly felt alone and unloved.
2) Remember, we are social beings. If one of your friends starts to withdraw from people, this could be a warning sign.
    - The best coping skill in this world is being with other people, the ability to talk to someone else.
3) Try to see their pain through their eyes. There is nothing worse than talking to a friend about your pain and having them downplay it or one-up it. Use empathy not sympathy. Empathy simply means feeling WITH the person.
4) Most importantly, we need a purpose in life as humans. Help find a purpose for their life. Get a vision; set some goals.

Remember, everything in life has happened for a reason to guide us, protect us, and strengthen us, so we can fulfill our purpose in life. People who are suicidal believe that the future is so painful that living is far worse than short-term pain of killing oneself.

Chapter Four
AMENDMENT 3

Forgiveness

Forgiveness will set you free. Don't let someone else have the power over you and hold you in bondage. Break the chains of misery and unforgiveness by forgiving them.

"True freedom can only be achieved through letting go of your own painful past and forgiving those whom you feel are unforgivable." (The great Colby Sutter)

I find this to be my biggest struggle in life, and I find this to be true in most people's lives. If we miss this topic, we miss the Gospel; we miss the very heart of God.

We first need to capture what I am about to say in order to get the rest of this message. Jesus summarizes the LAW as "LOVE your lord God with ALL your heart, soul, and strength." He then said, "Love your neighbor as you love yourself." (Luke 10:27)

I want you to write that statement out and say it every day when you wake up in the morning.

For example: I, Colby Sutter, love the Lord god with all my heart, soul, and strength. I love my neighbor as I love myself.

The New Testament gives us a commandment to live by. In Luke 10:25–28, the word of God is simple. It says:

> 25 On one occasion an expert in the law stood up to test Jesus. "Teacher," he asked, "what must I do to inherit eternal life?"
>
> 26 "What is written in the Law?" he replied. "How do you read it?"
>
> 27 He answered, "'Love the Lord your God with all your heart and with all your soul and with all your strength and with all your mind' and, 'Love your neighbor as yourself.'"
>
> 28 "You have answered correctly, "Jesus replied. "Do this and you will live."

Ask Yourself These Questions Please:

- Honestly, have I truly loved God with
    - All my heart?
    - All my mind?
    - With every thought?

1. With all my strength?
2. Do I love others as I do myself?
3. Do I care for them as I care for myself?
4. Am I concerned for them as I am concerned for myself?

Nobody can say yes to probably even one of those questions, let alone all of them. So we all have missed the mark on this commandment. If you do not believe me, let me quote Romans 3:23: "for all have sinned and fall shot of the glory of God."

5. Sin is everything that falls short of the Glory of God.

Unforgiveness is the complete opposite of love, the complete opposite of God's glory. If you want to be set free completely in this life from anything, then you need to pay attention to this amendment of forgiveness.

We are sinning against God—just let that sink into your brain for a second—if we have unforgiveness in our hearts. The Spirit told me to tell people to take this topic seriously. People water it down, but living in unforgiveness can cause sickness, separation from God, opening of the door to the devil, fruitlessness, unanswered prayers, and even death.

1John 3:14–15 explains it the best. It says:

> [14] We know that we have passed from death to life, because we love each other. Anyone who does not love remains in death. [15] Anyone who hates a brother or sister is a murderer, and you know that no murderer has eternal life residing in him.

Let me start off this topic with a few more questions that I want you to answer in the space provided. Please really think about these questions. Take a moment to pray and ask the Spirit of God to reveal the true answers.

1) Have you forgiven everyone in your life?

____

____

____

2) Who haven't you forgiven?

____

____

____

3) How do you know you have forgiven them?

____

____

____

As we move through, we will talk more about forgiveness. By the end of this chapter, I will teach you and show you how you can truly forgive that unforgivable person in your life.

"Forgive" means to give up resentment against or the desire to punish; it's a pardon, like cancelling a debt. Now think of all the people in your life and start to think if you really have forgiven them? You have to realize that unforgiveness can root itself inside of you. Once it did, it's hard to get it out. It produces hate, bitterness, and anger.

I found that most of my pain in life is due to my unforgiveness towards my dad. I've said I that I'd forgiven him many times to myself, but I never truly did. He was the hardest person in my life to forgive. I could have never done it on my own strength; it was completely God. God allowed me to forgive my father. He was an alcoholic who grew up being beaten by a father who did not show him any love, so he just reenacted what he learned growing up. When I was twelve, he took off, never to be seen again. There were no telephone calls or letters, nothing. He went to live his own life, leaving my mom, brother, and me behind. It is hard growing up fatherless.

Truth is that I had so much hatred for this man that it ate at me day in and day out. It got worse after age twenty. I wanted to kill him. I would get in fights and picture him as I hit people. I blamed him for my mom's death. I blamed him for my life of pain. I blamed him for my bad relationships with women. On my mom's deathbed, she made me promise that I would forgive my dad. I told her that I would and I tried to—but I did not, because I did not know how. I convinced myself that I had, but there was still pain and hatred inside of me. Finally, he came to Syracuse last year and wanted to meet me. My pastor told me to go, forgive him, pay him respect, and hear him out. After he left, I was angry and filled with rage and hatred—my unforgiveness was clear. Later, his mother (my grandmother) died, and he did not tell my brother or me about it. No one from his side of the family did. We only found out about it weeks later. So, naturally, my anger towards my father grew more and more. Fast-forward to New Year's Eve 2011 and the Spirit tells me to e-mail my dad and simply say, "I forgive you. Have a blessed New Year." That was it, short and sweet. I did not want to at first, and I put it off for hours. Finally, I thought of God and how God forgave me. Then I looked onto God, not my dad, and I sent the e-mail. Instantly, I felt lighter. For the first time in my life, I felt that I had truly forgiven him. I can now move on. Some people ask me about his reply.

"What did he say?"

And I said, "I do not know. The Lord told me not to worry or even read his reply—just e-mail him, forgive him, and go your own way." So I did. I used an e-mail account that I rarely use. I forgave him and just moved on without ever opening that account again. Just because you forgive a person does not mean you have to have a relationship with that person. *(Side note: From the time I'd been editing this book to the year 2014, I had coffee with him once and had a few e-mail conversations. It feels so good to be completely free from pain of the past and walk in complete forgiveness.)*

If you let unforgiveness into your life, it will grow and spread. Then it will kill your joy, steal your peace, and disrupt your spiritual life. Unforgiveness is a spiritual poison and can even affect your physical health.

We must love one another as Jesus has loved us (John 15:12). As a reminder, love is the exact opposite of unforgiveness. You cannot truly love somebody and hold grudge against him or her at the same time.

Jesus' parable about forgiveness is a great example.

Matthew 18:23–35

23 "Therefore, the kingdom of heaven is like a king who
wanted to settle accounts with his servants. 24 As he began the
settlement, a man who owed him ten thousand bags of gold
was brought to him. 25 Since he was not able to pay, the master
ordered that he and his wife and his children and all that he
had be sold to repay the debt.

26 "At this the servant fell on his knees before him. 'Be patient
with me,' he begged, 'and I will pay back everything.' 27 The
servant's master took pity on him, canceled the debt and
let him go.

28 "But when that servant went out, he found one of his fellow
servants who owed him a hundred silver coins. He grabbed
him and began to choke him. 'Pay back what you owe me!'
he demanded.

29 "His fellow servant fell to his knees and begged him, 'Be
patient with me, and I will pay it back.'

30 "But he refused. Instead, he went off and had the man
thrown into prison until he could pay the debt. 31 When the
other servants saw what had happened, they were outraged
and went and told their master everything that had happened.

32 "Then the master called the servant in. 'You wicked servant,'
he said, 'I canceled all that debt of yours because you begged
me to. 33 Shouldn't you have had mercy on your fellow servant
just as I had on you?' 34 In anger his master handed him over to
the jailers to be tortured, until he should pay back all he owed.

35 "This is how my heavenly Father will treat each of you unless
you forgive your brother or sister from your heart."

Meditate on this story and then write in the space provided what this parable means to you and what you learned from it.

____

____

____

____

____

Let's break this parable down a little. It says, "This is how my heavenly Father will treat each of you unless you forgive your brother or sister from your heart." Forgiveness is not just words to be spoken; it should come from the heart. It also says that unforgiveness causes torment. In Matthew 18:34 (NKJ), it says that "in anger the master delivered him to the jailers to be tortured." Unforgiveness opens you up to the tormentors. In verse 35, it says, "[S]o also my Heavenly Father will do to every one of YOU, if you do not forgive your brothers IN your HEART." That's the hard part. Not only do we have to forgive them in our hearts, but we also have to love them as Christ does. This is his command to us.

There's something interesting about this parable. The first servant owed ten thousand talents. That is equivalent to about 12 million dollars. This would have been impossible to pay back. So, basically, the king ordered that the servant, his wife, and his children be sold into slavery, and everything the servant owns be put up for sale. By doing so, the king could at least get some money back. This is why in verse 26 the servant was begging for mercy; he was literally pleading for his life. Then in verse 27, things took a complete 180-degree turn; a true miracle happened. Just when you thought it was all over for this servant—he was probably just about to give up and accept his defeat—the king totally forgave the debt. He cancelled it in its entirety. The servant got to keep his wife, children, and property. The loan was paid; they were completely free.

Put yourself in the servant's shoes for one moment. How would you feel right at that moment? Write it down. If you owed 12 million dollars and you were about to lose your family and all your possessions, and then the king forgave you and erased your debt, how would you feel?

By the way, that is what Jesus did for us: He paid our unpayable debt. He erased all of our debt and our sins. He is like this gracious king in this parable.

Now let's look at servant two. He owed servant one a hundred denarii. Fun fact: 100 denarii is equivalent today to ... are you ready? One dollar and eighty cents. According to the research I have done. That's right—one dollar and eighty cents.

> 28 "But that servant went out and found one of his fellow servants who owed him a hundred denarii; and he laid hands on him and took *him* by the throat, saying, 'Pay me what you owe!'"

Servant one shows no mercy at all, no forgiveness. Instead, he has servant two thrown into prison until he can work off the debt. After he was shown mercy on a debt that he could not pay back in his life, he went and turned around and did not forgive a debt for a dollar and eighty. This is similar to what happens to each of us today who are forgiven by Jesus but often refuse to forgive others. I know it is hard to forgive certain people, but I am telling you that it's not an option—we must forgive everyone. It is over for servant one and two. But luckily for us, it is not over if we listen to Christ and forgive others in our HEARTS. If not, we are going to wind up like servant one. It says so in verse 35.

Another very important fact about unforgiveness is that it can block God from answering prayers. When I first heard of it, I didn't believe it. So I researched this fact for myself. Let us read a few scriptures first so you can see what I am talking about.

Mark 11:24–25

> 24 Therefore I tell you, whatever you ask for in prayer, believe that you have received it, and it will be yours.
> 25 And when you stand praying, if you hold anything against anyone, forgive them, *so that* your *Father in heaven* may forgive ***you*** *your sins.*"

John 15: 5–10

> 5 "I am the vine; you are the branches. If you remain in me and I in you, you will bear much fruit; apart from me you can do
> nothing. 6 If you do not remain in me, you are like a branch that is thrown away and withers; such branches are picked
> up, thrown into the fire and burned. 7 If you remain in me and my words remain in you, ask whatever you wish, and it will be
> done for you. 8 This is to my Father's glory, that you bear much fruit, showing yourselves to be my disciples.
>
> 9 "As the Father has loved me, so have I loved you. Now remain
> in my love. 10 If you keep my commands, you will remain in my love, just as I have kept my Father's commands and remain in his love.

John 15 tells us that if we abide in Christ, we will produce spiritual fruit. The way to abide in Christ is by keeping his commandments. Verse 12 tells us that his commandment is to love one another as he has loved us. Therefore, if we do not love one another as he has loved us, we do not *abide* in him. So how are we supposed to produce spiritual fruit if we do not abide in him? According to verse 6, the branch that does not abide in the vine will be cast into the fire.

Verse 7 tells us that if we abide in him (by keeping his commandments) and his word in us, we can ask for anything, and it will be given onto us. So we love everyone as Christ loved us, and then realize that it cannot be authentic if we don't forgive. But if we love that person, we can expect all of our prayers answered. Forgiveness is the key.

Almost all bondages and chains can be broken when a person forgives those who have wronged them. Unforgiveness gives Satan an advantage, and we do not ever want to give Satan an advantage. We see this in 2 Corinthians 2:10–11.

> 10 When you forgive this man, I forgive him, too. And when I forgive whatever needs to be forgiven, I do so with Christ's authority for your benefit, 11 so that Satan will not outsmart us. For we are familiar with his evil schemes.

Matthew 6:14–15

> 14 For if you forgive other people when they sin against you, your heavenly Father will also forgive you. 15 But if you do not forgive others their sins, your Father will not forgive your sins.

To me this is one of the most powerful verses in the Bible, as well as one of the scariest. If you do not forgive others, then your Father will not forgive you.

Jesus had the ultimate reason not to forgive. He had the ultimate reason to want revenge, to harbor hatred and bitterness. But what did he do? Let's look at the book of Luke because it shows us, through Jesus, how we should act and forgive.

Luke 6:37

37 "Do not judge, and you will not be judged. Do not condemn, and you will not be condemned. Forgive, and you will be forgiven.

Luke 23: 34–43

34 Jesus said, "Father, ***forgive them, for they do not know what they are doing***." And they divided up his clothes by casting lots.

35 The people stood watching, and the rulers even sneered at him. They said, "He saved others; let him save himself if he is God's Messiah, the Chosen One."

36 The soldiers also came up and mocked him. They offered him
wine vinegar 37 and said, "If you are the king of the Jews, save
yourself."

38 There was a written notice above him, which read: THIS IS THE KING OF THE JEWS.

39 One of the criminals who hung there hurled insults at him: "Aren't you the Messiah? Save yourself and us!"

40 But the other criminal rebuked him. "Don't you fear God,"
he said, "since you are under the same sentence? 41 We are
punished justly, for we are getting what our deeds deserve. But
this man has done nothing wrong."

42 Then he said, "Jesus, remember me when you come into your kingdom."

43 Jesus answered him, "Truly I tell you, today you will be with me in paradise.

He didn't say he was going to kill everyone, or "Do you know who I am?" He simply said, "Father, forgive them, for they do not know what they are doing."

You and I are going to get knocked around in this life many times by many people. People are going to do us wrong. Some of them are going to come to us to ask for forgiveness. And some of them are going to be pretty awful people who have done awful things to us. Most of them, to us, will not *deserve* to be forgiven. But remember, you and I didn't *deserve* to be forgiven either.

As Christians, we are confronted with a choice (a choice that leads us further from or closer to God)—one that will set us free or keep us in bondage.

We can choose to:

1) Focus on the pain and our pride and withhold forgiveness, like servant one in the parable. We can wind up in a prison of anger, hatred, and depression—or being tortured. We will be filled with a life of unanswered prayers and have an unfruitful Christian life. At our death, we will look at Jesus and hear him say, "I forgave you, but why didn't you forgive this person? I commanded you to forgive others as I have forgiven you!"

OR

2) Forgive and be set free.

Now let's answer an important question that you are most likely thinking. We talked about the importance of forgiving people and how it is a heart issue, and what happens if we do not forgive. This time let's talk about how to forgive.

How to Forgive

1) **Speak to the Root of the Unforgiveness in Your Heart**
   a. Your voice represents your authority; therefore, when you raise your voice, you release your authority.
      i. Your thoughts alone will not remove these poisonous roots in your life.
      ii. If you do not speak to your emotions, they will speak to you.
      iii. If you do not take authority over your emotions, they will take authority over you.
      iv. If you do not rise up and conquer your flesh, it will rise up and conquer you.
   b. Take command and own your thoughts.

You have to treat bitterness, resentment, and unforgiveness like they are the enemy coming to corrupt your soul. Think of it as a foe trying to kill you emotionally and physically, because it is. Wage war on unforgiveness.

If you want to be set free, it's going to take an attitude that says, "I'm going to get to the root of this beast and yank it from my soul. I'm not going to stop until I am totally free."

You need to look at who God is and what God has done for you instead of looking at the person you are trying to forgive and what he or she has done to you—because you can't forgive that way.

2) **Pray**
   a. Do you want to forgive someone or stop your feeling of hatred for someone? Pray for them every day. Pray to God to bless that person, to fill his or her needs, and to fill him or her with joy. Pray for these every day for a few weeks and watch your heart turn towards that person.

b. You can't hate someone and pray for them to be blessed at the same time. (Remember, God knows your heart when you are praying.)

How can I tell if I have forgiven someone?

You know you have forgiven someone when you stop talking about that person or telling people the story of what they did to you. If you are sounding like this, "I forgave them, but this one time they did this. But I forgave them," then in your heart you did not truly forgive them because to forgive is to wipe clean. You will always remember, but the pain associated with it will be gone. Therefore, there will be no need to relive it by retelling "the story."

Unforgiveness can separate us from God and destroy us. If we truly love Christ and want Him to forgive us, we must follow His command and love each other, so that we will not have any unforgiveness in our hearts towards anyone.

There is someone this very day who needs to hear you say, "I forgive you," not just with your mouth but with your heart. Do this and I promise you that you are well on your way to true freedom. Forgiving others will set you free.

Scriptures

Matthew 6:14–15

In prayer there is a connection between what God does and what you do. You can't get forgiveness from God, for instance, without also forgiving others. If you refuse to do your part, you cut yourself off from God's part.

1 John 1:9

On the other hand, if we admit our sins—make a clean breast of them—he won't let us down; he'll be true to himself. He'll forgive our sins and purge us of all wrongdoing.

Isaiah 43:25–26

"But I, yes I, am the one who takes care of your sins—that's what I do. I don't keep a list of your sins. "So, make your case against me. Let's have this out. Make your arguments. Prove you're in the right.

Acts 3:19

Now it's time to change your ways! Turn to face God so he can wipe away your sins, pour out showers of blessing to refresh you.

Isaiah 1:18

"Come. Sit down. Let's argue this out." This is God's Message: "If your sins are blood-red, they'll be snow-white. If they're red like crimson, they'll be like wool."

2 Corinthians 5:17

Now we look inside, and what we see is that anyone united with the Messiah gets a fresh start, is created new. The old life is gone; a new life burgeons! Look at it!

Ephesians 1:7

Because of the sacrifice of the Messiah, his blood poured out on the altar of the Cross, we're a free people—free of penalties and punishments chalked up by all our misdeeds. And not just barely free, either. Abundantly free!

Hebrews 10:17

He concludes, I'll forever wipe the slate clean of their sins.

Daniel 9:9

Compassion is our only hope, the compassion of you, the Master, our God, since in our rebellion we've forfeited our rights.

Colossians 1:13–14

God rescued us from dead-end alleys and dark dungeons. He's set us up in the kingdom of the Son he loves so much, the Son who got us out of the pit we were in, got rid of the sins we were doomed to keep repeating.

Psalm 103:12

And as far as sunrise is from sunset, he has separated us from our sins.

Numbers 14:19–21

"Please forgive the wrongdoing of this people out of the extravagance of your loyal love just as all along, from the time they left Egypt, you have been forgiving this people." God said, "I forgive them, honoring your words. But as I live and as the Glory of God fills the whole Earth."

Micah 7:18–19

Where is the god who can compare with you—wiping the slate clean of guilt, turning a blind eye, a deaf ear, to the past sins of your purged and precious people? You don't nurse your anger and don't stay angry long, for mercy is your specialty. That's what you love most. And compassion is on its way to us. You'll stamp out our wrongdoing. You'll sink our sins to the bottom of the ocean.

Matthew 6:9–15

With a God like this loving you, you can pray very simply, like this: Our Father in heaven, reveal who you are. Set the world right; Do what's best—as above, so below. Keep us alive with three square meals. Keep us forgiven with you and forgiving others. Keep us safe from ourselves and the Devil. You're in charge! You can do anything you want! You're ablaze in beauty! Yes. Yes. Yes. In prayer there is a connection between what God does and what you do. You can't get forgiveness from God, for instance, without also forgiving others. If you refuse to do your part, you cut yourself off from God's part.

Mark 11:25

And when you assume the posture of prayer, remember that it's not all asking. If you have anything against someone, forgive—only then will your heavenly Father be inclined to also wipe your slate clean of sins.

Matthew 26:28

This is my blood, God's new covenant poured out for many people for the forgiveness of sins.

Chapter Five
Amendment 4

Guard Your Mouth (Speak No Evil)

"Death and life are in the power of the tongue and they that love it shall eat the fruit thereof."
Proverbs 18:21

We have all heard of the three monkeys—see no evil, speak no evil, and hear no evil. The origin of these monkeys is seventeenth-century Japan. The monkey covering his eyes is sees no evil; the one covering his ears is hears no evil; and the one covering his mouth is speaks no evil. There are various meanings, but basically I believe they represent being of good mind, speech, and action. Amendment 4 is a biblical principle loosely based on the concept of speak no evil. The Lord gave me an image of armed soldiers guarding my mouth who are not allowing certain things to be said out from my lips. This concept is so powerful, because I truly believe that the words of your mouth can either bring life or death to you. The words of your mouth can manifest if you are filled with joy, love, and peace or with hopelessness, fear, and anger.

In this chapter, I will cover how I used to talk by using some personal stories and how that way of speech affected me emotionally and physically. Then I will give you the actual rules the Lord gave me to fulfill this step. Lastly, I will provide Bible scriptures about this topic on guarding your mouth.

I think we take our free speech for granted. It feels as if we talk without even thinking of what we are truly saying. When I spoke at schools, one thing I would say to the students was that they will attract things in their life that they continually talk about. "Can you prove this?" you may be asking as you sit there reading this. Yes I can. They have websites, books, and seminars on this topic. All you have to do is google "the power of positive speech." The Old Testament even talks about how words have power, and that the proper use of them requires wisdom. However, instead of using those examples, I am going to share what actually happened to me as evidence of how this principle actually works.

When I was in first grade, my dad used to call me "the toughest kid in the neighborhood"; that was my nickname. Other kids began to call me this way that I began to call myself this way. Other family members even said that about me. It became my mind-set and eventually my self-image. I truly started to believe I was the toughest kid in the neighborhood and carried myself like that. Little did I know at this age that a cursed prophecy I would live out was put on me; I adopted that image. I began to get in a lot of fights at school. Why? Because I was the toughest kid in the neighborhood. It got so bad that I felt a sense of entitlement to do whatever I wanted and go wherever I wanted. One weekend, I was outside setting up a tent with a few other friends, including my neighbor who was sixteen at the time. He and my older brother were setting up their tent. Well, I decided that I wanted to play in that one, but I was told no. So I insisted. I even began to walk into the tent. My neighbor stood up and pushed me back, saying, "You're not going in." What did I do? Being the toughest kid in the neighborhood, I started to fight the sixteen-year-old. Needless to say, he broke two bones in my wrist. The pain hurt so bad that I remember passing out on my way to the emergency room. I could have also passed out from the whisky my dad gave me as a pain killer, but that is a different story. Nevertheless, my confession of being the toughest kid in the neighborhood became my reality, right along with the consequences. Speaking of consequence, remember this as a life lesson. You are free to choose whatever you want in life, but you are not free to choose your consequences.

Confessions can be dangerous. If we spend enough time confessing the wrong things in our life, it will eventually produce fruit. My confession of being tough was my image; that was who I was. That is why I became a bouncer at night clubs and bars. I took a job working with inmates in a federal community correction facility. Whenever I felt challenged or disrespected, even at work, I would fight; fists were always my first option. When I was bouncing, if someone got out of line, I would be the first on the scene. I would usually headbutt the person or choke them. I loved this image of being tough. I would even call myself the toughest kid in the neighborhood at times when I became an adult. These behaviors started to grow from inside of me and kill the spiritual side of me. No wonder I was so miserable. When I eventually came back to the church, I had all this lifelong evil inside of me that would not disappear.

From as early as I can remember, I used to confess to my mom that I was going to be in the Mafia. I would tell her I was going to be a gangster and buy her a house one day. You may read this and laugh, but I am serious. I would confess this *all* the time for years and years until I was in my early twenties. My mom would laugh, thinking it was a big joke. However, she didn't know I meant it. I truly wanted to be in the Mafia from as long as I can remember. When I was a kid, my mom and dad would have me say it to other people. Their friends would come over, and they would ask what I wanted to be when I grew up. I would tell them, "I want to be in the Mafia," or "I want to be a gangster." It got to the point where

I would watch movies over and over again about the Mafia, and I would always root for the bad guys to win. I would read books about the Mafia. I would lie in bed and fantasize about the Mafia and working for the Mafia. When I started to sell drugs, I started to think I was on my way to becoming what I've been confessing over all these years. As I sold more drugs, I started to recruit friends and act like we were family, like we were Mafia. By ninth grade, I started my first gang. And let me get this clear. For the record, it was not a real gang; it was a group of four friends with a name, and we thought we were cool. We broke into cars, stole, robbed, and sold drugs. And anyone of us probably would have ratted each other out at this time if ever caught by the police. That was only the beginning.

I was connected to "connected" people, those who would take trips to Italy, New Jersey, or New York City on a regular basis. They are people who would give me hundreds of dollars without thinking twice. They would and could take away certain problems in your life and have certain people end up missing. I would hang out with these people every day. I started to do favors for these friends of mine. In return, I was untouchable. I did and got whatever I wanted; I was family to them. I looked back at this point in my life and noticed that I came as close as I could to what I had been confessing since I was a child. I was taught by these friends of mine not to talk on the phone or talk to people. We did not know about anything. They, too, followed this principle of guarding the mouth from a nonspiritual perspective. Even though this was a worldly concept to me now, I still guarded every word out of my mouth and never spoke over the phone about anything that could hurt me. I never spoke to people; I did not know about anything. This same principle of guarding your mouth is what God wants us to do concerning fruitful positive confessions. In dealing with my "family," my mouth could have and did keep me out of prison, but it could have put me in prison for a very long time. You need to think of the power of your mouth. Treat each word you speak out of it as if it is life-giving, because it is. Or you can speak negative confessions, leading to your loss of freedom and even death.

Another example is when my best friend and I started our very own rap group. We played all over—in clubs, bars, parties, and talent shows. We even made CDs and videos. The things I would rap about were so filled with hatred and pain. I became more and more miserable, not only because I was confessing negative things all the time, but I was also *listening* to my own confessions on a regular basis. I wish I knew this at the time; however, I did not. The lifestyle quickly became addicting—the fans, the cheering, the complements, the money for one night of fun, the free drinks, the parties, and the image of saying how tough you are in your songs then having to back it up all the time. At that time, I was so lost, but I thought I loved what I was doing. It's amazing looking back now at the things I said. Some lines in my songs were:

"I am like a Rottweiler stuck up in a cage, with rage.
Nothing good ever comes this way,
So I stay taking in the bad, waiting on the 12 rounds with dad."

I took out the swear words in that line. Every song was about suicide, anger, or drugs.

"Hell's got me restless,
Close to death and breathless.
I can't eat when I slit my wrist. I can't sleep.
If I am doctor Jekyll, where is Mr. Hyde?
Please, God, forgive me. Is it my turn to die?
I pop pills to kill these voices in my head."

"I can't sleep at night,
Because all these voices might
Push me to one day try to take my life."

These are just a few lines out of hundreds of songs we made over the years. In this part of my life, all I wanted is to die, fight, or drink liquor mixed with some pain pills. I created my reality, just like my dad created the toughest boy in the neighborhood into existence. All with words.

This principle of guarding your mouth works for positive as well as it does for negative. Let me share two more examples of how God used this amendment in my life. I was driving a car that would not pass inspection. As a result, I had to drop out of graduate school, because the school was on a military base and therefore ID and inspection sticker were checked every time one is pulling onto the grounds. So, here I am working, going to church, speaking at church events, volunteering with youth, and my car was a death trap that broke down almost as much as it ran. I had no extra money to buy a car; I didn't even have a down payment for a used car. I had nothing in my bank. One day, after hearing a church service message about standing on faith, I got motivated in the spirit to try something. I went home, prayed, and had a talk with my Heavenly Father. I felt that he wanted to give me a car, and so I tried to reason with him and get the specifics on how he wanted to bless me. I felt a strong conviction, saying, "No, I want to *give* you a car." So I finished my prayer by thanking God for the car he was going to give me even though I had not received it yet. This started a pattern of faith building. Every morning, I would wake up and say, "Lord, thank you for my car." Every evening before bed, I would say, "Lord, thank you for my car." I believe He was actually going to give me a car, that I already received it because he said it was so. Even though I did not possess it or see it yet, I knew it was mine, because God said it was. This is why I did not pray every day for a car. I prayed it once, and then thanked him every day for it. I did not tell anyone of what I was doing because I did not want to influence someone to try to help me; this was between me and God. The only thing I would say, for example, is that I was driving a teen home after a mentoring event.

He said to me, "Man, you need a new car. Why don't you buy one?"

I replied, "I am getting one. God is taking care of it."

I would only speak positive things into my future regarding the car. Sometimes you have to *see* the vision you want before you can get it.

In order to see my vision, I cut out the car I wanted—the year, the color, and even the type of rims. I hung it up at my desk at work and on my door at home. Every time I walked by it, I would thank God for my car. A few months passed and I finally get a phone call. A buddy of mine called me up and said, "We have car down here that would be perfect for you. It's only a couple of years old. Come down and check it out."

So I drove down there and I loved it. It was in great shape. I asked, "How much?"

He said, "Give me a grand down, and then you can make payments."

I did not have a grand! So I decided that we need to *help* God along. He generated a receipt saying I put three thousand down as a deposit. He did this so I could go to my bank and try to get a loan for a grand and show them I already have some of my own money invested in this car. Even though it was a lie, I decided to do it. I went to my credit union, sat with a loan officer, and asked for a thousand dollars. I explained why I needed it, how I would pay it back, and even told them, "I have direct deposit with you guys. You can just take it out of my account when I get paid." They left the room for a little while. I prayed to God, "Please let me get this car. I need it. It is perfect for me. Please, God, thank you." In my head this was the deal. This was perfect. In my own mind, everything added up. About an hour later, I was with the loan officer again, and she told me that the bank declined my request for a thousand dollars. She said she was sorry, but I was too high risk. Very disappointed, I left hurt, angry, and defeated. I got into my car and drove away.

In my spirit, I heard God said, "I told you, son, I was going to *give* you a car."

I woke up the next day, and I did not thank God for my car. I was too defeated, too upset. About a week passed and I'd completely stopped thanking Him for my car. I gave up this silly notion that God was going to give me a car and that He was magically going to come down from heaven, ring my doorbell, and stand on my porch with a pair of keys in His hand. After about three weeks of my pity party, I was driving to work seven thirty in the morning, and I started to pray. I heard God said aloud in my Spirit, "Aren't you going to thank me for your car today?"

So I mustered the strength to actually say it. I once again said a positive confession of what was going to happen according to God. I said, "Lord, thank you so much for the car you gave me. I love it. Thank you."

I got to my office and worked the entire day. When I got home, I started to write sermon for an event. At six that evening, the phone rang, and it was a man I know. He said to me, "Colby, I was walking, and the Lord told me to give you the car in my parking lot. Can you come down and pick it up this week?"

I asked, "What do you want for it?"

He said, "Nothing. It is yours. God wants to give it to you."

But this is my favorite part of the story. I'd just put my last twenty-five dollars in my car for gas the day before. I had no money, and I was driving to pick up my car that God got for me. I said to myself, "Man, I wish I hadn't wasted my money on gas yesterday. I hope I have enough to at least get the car home."

The moment I was about to pick up the car, the guy told me, "By the way, I felt led to fill up the gas tank for you as well, so you have a full tank of gas." He then handed me the keys, and I drove home.

God is amazing and will bless you. You just have to stand in faith and confess His blessings. The power of positive confessions is amazing. The last story I will share about positive confession is about a job I had. It actually took place probably six months after I was blessed with a car.

I was working as a gambling prevention specialist, and one day I got called into the director's office. He said to me, "Your job is being eliminated at the end of the year."

I was not the only one losing my job. Everyone across New York State who did what I do was losing their jobs. There were about three months left in the year. I said, "No problem, and thank you for the heads up." I went back to my office started to put my resume together. I thought of where I should apply, what kind of job I wanted—things like that. Finally, I decided to pray. I then felt in my spirit once again that God had this under control. I felt that I was not supposed to look for a job. I was to do nothing but trust in him and keep working at the job I am doing now. So I did just that. I did not look for one job. I did not think about it. I just prayed and trusted in God. Coworkers would come into my office and say how sorry they were that my job was going to be cut and ask what I was going to do. I would say, "God has it under control."

About two months, I got called back into my director's office. He said to me, "OK, next month, your job is going to be cut, so we are going to let you go today. But we would like to offer you this new job with a five-thousand-dollar raise."

I took the new job with the raise and said, "Thank you."

My coworkers said, "You showed no emotion at all. Why not?"

I said, "I already knew that my God had it taken care of. He told me not to worry. He has it all under control." Once again faith mixed with positive confessions gives God something to work with. Try and watch what miracles God has for you.

Below are the actual rules and steps God gave me about guarding your mouth.

Freedom Exercises

Step One: Guard Your Mouth

First, you need to watch what you say and confess; you need to actually take notice. Write it down if you have to when you say negative things about yourself, even whenever you think negative things. Document them; this will force you to take notice of your thought pattern. You can break your thought pattern easier if you take notice of it. This works best if you can do this right after it happens, but if you can't, you can wait to the end of the day and write them down as you reflect on your day. Also, write down where you were and what you were doing. This will help you notice if there is a pattern or not, a pattern you can easily start to change.

1) Write down all your negative confessions and thoughts for the week:
   a. Monday:

      ____

      ____

      ____

   b. Tuesday:

      ____

      ____

      ____

   c. Wednesday:

      ____

      ____

      ____

d. Thursday:

___

___

___

e. Friday:

___

___

___

f. Saturday:

___

___

___

g. Sunday:

___

___

___

2) Write down the location and what you were doing at the time of each negative confession and thought. For example, you said, "I am broke; I will never pay off my bills this year," every time. You'd notice that you said it three times this week and every time after you received a phone call from a bill collector. That is the pattern. You receive a call, then you speak negative. Now you know you need to not only change your confession, but also be aware that when that phone rings, you may be tested. So break the pattern and have positive confessions ready to be used as you hang up that phone.

a. Monday:

___

___

___

b. Tuesday:

____

____

____

c. Wednesday:

____

____

____

d. Thursday:

____

____

____

e. Friday:

____

____

____

f. Saturday:

____

____

____

g. Sunday:

____

____

____

Second, confess good things that you are standing in faith for and positive things about yourself every day. Confess them every morning, afternoon, and evening. You need to say positive things about yourself for the rest of your life. Say them out loud. Wake up and say, "Thank you, God, for another day. God, thank you for today. I am happy and full of joy. Thank you for the people in my life who will go out of their way to bless me. I have supernatural favor throughout the day. I am blessed and highly favored._*I am God's favorite child.*" No matter what happens, do not speak negative things anymore. Always speak positivity and blessings towards any situation. This will bring about victory. You should write positive things about yourself and read them every day. Write what you believe for and confess them every day as if you already have them. I have sticky notes all over my house with positive sayings and things I believe for. So every time I walk by them, I can read them out loud and confess them.

Now I want you to write down three positive things about yourself. Next, write three things that you believe God will do in your life. Then I want you to write down Bible verses for each one to support what you wrote. Rewrite the Bible verse in present tense and make it personal to you. You are going to read these out loud every day until you get what you believe and you are convinced you are the positive things you wrote about yourself.

Example: (Let's say I am sick and believe for healing.)

I have energy all day long, and no sickness can enter my body. I feel great and healthy today

Bible Verse:

Jeremiah 30:17: "For I will restore health to you, and your wounds will be healed," declares the Lord.

Translation:

God has restored health to me; all my wounds are healed because the Lord has declared this.

Positive Things about Yourself:

1) ____
____
2) ____
____
3) ____
____

Bible Verses:

1) ____
____
2) ____
____
3) ____
____

Translation:

1) ____
____
2) ____
____
3) ____
____

Three Things You Believe God For:

1) ____
____
2) ____
____
3) ____
____

Bible Verses:

1) ____
____
2) ____
____
3) ____
____

Translation:

1) ____
____
2) ____
____
3) ____
____

Scriptures

If you are looking for some great Bible verses to support everything I just said about guarding your mouth, these are a few of my favorites. I suggest that you read these out loud every day.

Psalm 141:3

Set a guard, O Lord, before my mouth; keep watch at the door of my lips.

- To set a guard – to watch over, protect, defend, keep from escaping or from trouble, to control or restrain

In this verse, you are actually asking the Lord to watch over and protect your mouth over every single word that comes out of it. Try to imagine Jesus guarding your mouth. Picture your mouth as a door with the lips open and words are coming out of it. Jesus is the almighty protector of your mouth, and he is watching every word. "Lord, keep watch at the door of my lips. Keep negative words from escaping; control my words, Lord."

In my entire life, I boxed and at times even taught boxing. The first thing I teach is guard. A boxer gets in his stance and sets up his guard. Why is the guard so important? It keeps you from getting hit in the face. If you get hit, not only does the opponent get points for each hit, but he can eventually hit you hard enough and take you out of the match. If you do not have a guard in boxing, you will never win any fights and will just get hurt. Your guard protects you; it allows you to get in position by deflecting and tiring out your opponent. You'll often see tired boxers relax their guard. Such as in life, you start to get tired, worn out, or frustrated, and you drop your guard and start talking in a defeated manner. A good corner man (the word of God) will yell at you, "Keep your guard up!" When you read this verse, I want you to picture yourself as a boxer (there you are in your boxing stance with your guard up ready to fight). "Set a guard, O Lord." Your mouth is now a fine-tuned, well-trained fighter that only allows words that build you up and not tear your down.

James 1:26

If any of you consider himself religious and yet does not keep a tight rein on his tongue, he deceives himself and his religion is worthless.

- Religious – piously observant of the external duties of his faith
- Worthless – without worth, futile, barren, useless

What we say are verbal expressions of our souls. We need to bring our mouth to the Lord and have it submitted to him.

Psalm 34:13

Keep your tongue from evil and your lips from speaking lies.

Proverbs 13:3

He who guards his lips guards his life, but he who speaks rashly will become to ruin.

Proverbs 21:23

He who guards his mouth and his tongue keeps himself from disaster.

Matthew 12:34

You brood of vipers, how can you who are evil say anything good? For out of the overflow of the heart the mouth speaks.

Chapter Six
Amendment 5

Guard Your Ears and Eyes (Hear No Evil, See No Evil)

This is closely related to chapter five, which discussed guarding your mouth (speak no evil). In this chapter, we will discuss guarding your ears and eyes, which both receive information; they work as receptors. Just like I said the words of your mouth bring life and death, what you watch and listen to could also bring spiritual life and death. It can rob you of your joy, hope, and future. What you hear and watch can shape your life and redirect your path, change your morals, bring you into captivity, and nurture pride, which can separate you from God. I will talk about how music influenced me in life, past and present. I will talk about the movies I watched that influenced my thinking patterns and the way I acted. I will share statistics about violence and the role media plays in those stats. Then I will share with you what the Lord told me to do regarding my ears and eyes.

Hear No Evil:

List your top seven (7) favorite songs or bands:

1. ____________________
2. ____________________
3. ____________________
4. ____________________
5. ____________________
6. ____________________
7. ____________________

Later, in your spare time, take a moment to listen to the songs—I mean, really listen to the song or songs those bands play—and list the theme. Then list the overall message, words used, topic, emotions—things like that.

1. ____________________
2. ____________________
3. ____________________
4. ____________________
5. ____________________
6. ____________________
7. ____________________

Words are very powerful. This is why we must guard our ears. Words and sound can set the mood. Our minds react differently to different sounds and words. We hear a gentle sound of water dripping into a creek. This sound may produce an emotion different from hearing a jackhammer in front of your house. In other words, certain sounds and words cause us to feel differently. This is even truer for music, because music put together the sound and the words to set a mood. We will discuss more on this in a few minutes. Sound has been proven to help us relieve stress, create a deep sense of well-being, and promote health. According to a study

I read, sound therapy is being used all over the world because of the healing power of sounds. *"From playing Bach in the nursery to yogic chanting in the oncologist's office, sound therapy is gaining popularity as both a preventative medicine and as a complement to more-traditional treatments. Good for both the mind and the body, it has been shown to help lift depression, clear sinuses and help cancer patients recover more quickly from chemotherapy,"* ("Wellness," by Karen Olson/November 2006, https://experiencelife.com). For years, people have been using sounds and human voices in forms of chanting for healing. This concept is not new.

According to an article in the *New York Times, "Healers, sometimes called sounders, argue that sound can have physiological effects because its vibrations are not merely heard but also felt. And vibrations, they say, can lower heart rate variability, relax brain wave patterns and reduce respiratory rates."*

Sound therapy decreases stress. This is good news for everyone, but most especially for people with serious illness. Before I go on to personal examples, I want to share a story with you. This story sums up the power negative words can have on you.

Negative Words Have Power

There once was a bunch of tiny frogs who arranged a running competition. The goal was to reach the top of a very high tower. A big crowd had gathered around the tower to see the race and cheer on the contestants.

The race began. Honestly, no one in the crowd really believed that the tiny frogs would reach the top of the tower. You would hear statements such as:

"Oh, WAY too difficult!"

"They will NEVER make it to the top."

"Not a chance that they will succeed. The tower is too high!"

The tiny frogs began collapsing one by one, except for those who in a fresh tempo were climbing higher and higher.

The crowd continued to yell, "It is too difficult! No one will make it!"

More tiny frogs got tired and gave up, but ONE continued higher and higher and higher. This one wouldn't give up!

At the end, everyone else had given up climbing the tower, except for the one tiny frog who—after a big effort—was the only one who reached the top!

THEN all of the other tiny frogs naturally wanted to know how this one frog managed to do it.

A contestant asked the tiny frog how he had found the strength to succeed and reach the goal.

It turned out that the winner was DEAF!

The wisdom of this story is: Never listen to other people's tendencies to be negative or pessimistic because they take your most wonderful dreams and wishes away from you—the ones you have in your heart!

Always think of the power words have because everything you hear and read will affect your actions!

Therefore, ALWAYS be POSITIVE! And above all, be DEAF when people tell YOU that you cannot fulfill your dreams!

(I did not write this story. I am not sure who did. I got this story sent to me years ago in a chain e-mail.)

Growing up, music played an indescribable role in my life. Being in one form of musical group or another, I have found that I cannot do anything without music playing in the background. What I love most about music is the words. I am a word guy. I am the type who will rewind a song ten times just to make sure I heard each and every word. The music I gravitated to was gangster rap music. The more violent and angry the music, the more I loved it. I would listen for hours learning each and every word, then later confess the words out loud over and over again. Before I knew it, I started to feel angrier. I started to feel more and more like a gangster and became what I was listening to. If you keep hearing over and over again that it is "OK" to act a certain way and talk a certain way, you start to think it is acceptable. Not only did I think it was OK when I started to sell drugs at a young age, but I also thought it was cool. I thought it was how you become a man and how you gain respect. That distorted belief continued to influence me when I got older. What I listened to connected with my heart and soul, giving me the false impression that what I was doing was "right." If you asked me back then—when I was an educated college graduate—who I respected more, the president of the United States or the richest, most gangster drug dealer, I would have answered, "The drug dealer." This is how I had proven that it has nothing to do with education level, but has all to do with what you allow to influence your life.

Pride starts to grow in you when you become self-conceited. You begin to look down on someone because of education, social status, or even spiritual status. You begin to think that you achieve your success because of you and you alone. And you are proud of what you did and who you become. This makes me think of an angel who lost his place in heaven. Satan was the worship leader in heaven. His voice was like no one ever heard before, and his appearance was compared to precious stones. But because of his status, pride took root in him, and he began to challenge God's authority. For that, he earned God's wrath and was banished in heaven. If Satan, a worship leader who brings music in heaven, fell because of pride, what other conclusions can you draw? Worldly music is filled with pride. It is all about self; it is all about being the best of the best with the most amount of money. It is about coming from nothing and becoming a "somebody" all by yourself—without help from anyone. Satan rules the world. Of course, it makes sense that our culture and media—in fact, the rest of the world—is filled with pride. *"In their case the god of this world has blinded the minds of the unbelievers, to keep them from seeing the light of the gospel of the glory of Christ, who is the image of God"* (1 Corinthians 4:4, ESV).

Pride influences certain worldly music, which in turn affects the way some people act, feel, speak, and think. Before you know it, we are acting like the rest of the world. We bring forth evil and good things by what we speak. This is why "guarding your ears" is such an important step to freedom. Check what you are listening and what you are watching. The very message that influences you may alienate you from the God's grace. Remember that God hates pride. Let me share with you a journal entry about media and pride that I wrote while in prayer. It was at a time when I was already walking with the Lord and I thought everything was going great.

I've been walking with God for awhile now, and things have been going great. He has been showing me so much. I have been learning and growing. It is as if he has been holding my hand and talking with me, teaching me, guiding me. I've been so blessed. I have such a long way to go, but at least I can see how blessed I am. I have felt his love for the first time in years every day. I wake up happy and go to bed happy. I feel like I belong.

But as I grow to the next level, God has opened my eyes even more, and I thank him for that. For the last few weeks, I have been miserable. I haven't felt God around me. I haven't wanted to be around him. I've been dried up, thinking of death again, hating life, waiting to die or commit suicide, wanting to hurt people, rob people, beat people. I am yelling at people, angry, and jealous. My old desires to sell drugs started to come back. The desire to do drugs has come back. I actually took a few pain pills the other day. I knew I was turning my back on God, but I did it anyway. The desire to sin, the desire to be feared again, to have power again, to make people afraid of me, to use women, to get back at old girlfriends who hurt me in the past, to be a gangster and a hustler again—all these desires that God delivered me from have come back. Church people began to annoy me. The fake ones make me want to hit them, and I didn't want to be around the "real" ones.

I thought I was further along in my walk with God. I thought all those desires had been defeated and were gone. I can honestly tell you that for years now, none of these thoughts even crossed my mind. The sad part is that I saw this coming. God warned me of this a few times. And even though I saw it coming, I opened the door slowly, thinking "I can handle it." I thought I was strong enough. The first step to opening this door was media—music. I started listening to worldly music again. I become worldly. I'm not speaking against all secular music. But that music, those artists, songs that rekindle the "old" you—those remind me of selfish/negative desires or past hurts. This is what I returned to. Luckily, God opened my eyes before I fell too hard. I'd just slipped a little. For a short period, I felt all alone again. God used this to open my eyes.

When you start walking in the world and talking like the world, it is when you start walking in pride again. For me, music is the most dangerous thing. As soon as I started listening to worldly music again, my mood and my desires changed, causing my actions to change.

I love rap music. It speaks to me; it motivates me. I had to realize that some rap music, just like most forms of music, is fueled by pride. These artists embrace the following attitude: it's all about ME, being the hardest gangster there is, the best artist there is, the richest, the best of the best. It is wrapped in pride, and God hates pride. As soon as I started to listen to my favorite rap artist, I felt my pride start to come back. I felt God just left me. His presence just left, as if He said, "I am out of here." (Now God will never actually leave you, but this is how I felt.)

The "old" Colby was returning, but Christ said that we are new creations in Him. He also warns us about leaving our first love—Him. And I was doing just that by resurrecting a lifestyle and image that I had once lived vicariously through music. If country music is your thing, think of how the lyrics are consumed with alcoholism, abuse, and womanizing. If emo music is more your style, consider how that genre speaks of loneliness, isolation, death, and despair. Get my point? (Your heart will become proud, and you will forget the LORD your God [Deuteronomy 8:14].)

"Forget the Lord your God," that verse says. I want you to take some time right now and pounder that verse. Mediate on the word "forget." The verse says, "… you will forget the LORD your God." Pride is so powerful that it will take over your heart, and you will leave behind God in your daily activities.

Forget – To cease or fail to remember; be unable to recall: to forget someone's name. To leave behind unintentionally; neglect to take.

You will not even know you are doing this. You start to listen to certain music and watch certain movies with prideful themes. Pride then sneaks in a little at a time, and before you know it, you will fail to remember things about God. You are unable to recall what he has done for you. You feel alone, scared, hurt, depressed, and angry because you unintentionally left behind what matters most in your life, God.

As soon as I started to listen to some old rap songs, I started to listen to my type of music—hard core rap music. I started to dress back to my old way, lowering my eyes, walking with a strut and a chip on my shoulder. I started to say the lines out loud, and before I know it, I felt like I was "back." After a week of listening to nothing but gangster rap, I was hard as a rock again. All I wanted was to do drugs, sell drugs, fight, and start my rap group again, so people would know my name and who I was again. I wanted people to fear me, because to me, fear brought respect. It's amazing how fast and comfortable you can fall back into your old self. I welcomed myself back with open arms.

No matter what type of music you are listening to, its words will inspire you one way or another. Look at Hitler. His words inspired an entire country to believe in what he was saying. You can be inspired for good or evil. Music can inspire you to think you are stronger than everyone, better, "respected," or entitled, just like what my favorite quote in schools I hear all the time implies, "You don't know me." You may not even know that this is a form of pride, but it is. When you think you can beat up everyone you come in to contact with, that is pride. When you think people should fear you and give you respect, that is pride. When you say to yourself that this guy has no idea who I am or what I could do to him, that is pride.

God Hates Pride

Proverbs 16:5

English Translation: "Everyone who is arrogant in heart is an abomination to the Lord." Abomination means, disgrace, horror, evil, crime.

Amplified: "Everyone proud and arrogant in heart is disgusting, hateful and exceedingly offensive to the Lord."

Message Bible: "God can't stomach arrogance or pretense."

Proverbs 8:13

Message Bible: "Whose ways I hate with passion—pride and arrogance and crooked talk."

Amplified: "The reverent fear and worshipful awe of the Lord includes the hatred of evil; pride, arrogance, the evil way, and perverted and twisted speech I hate."

So if He hates it, and you are walking in it, do not think God will tolerate it. I am telling you firsthand that he will pull away from you. I am not saying leave you, but you will not feel his presence, and you will feel all alone.

When I was young, I was proud; it was all about being feared and respected. Now that I am in schools all the time doing presentations, I noticed that every kid I come across with and every adult I come in contact with is prideful. Pride is a cancer in our world. We cannot let it into our hearts and into our lives as Christians.

In everything you do in life, ask yourself, "Why am I doing this?" This will get down to the route of your actions. I am warning you: you do not see pride coming in most cases; you do not even have a clue that you have pride in your heart until you really break it down and look at it.

Ask yourself why you dress the way you do, why you hang out with certain people, why you talk like you do, why you listen to a certain type of music, why you go to church, why you dress a certain way while you're at church, why you look in the mirror sixteen times a day. Do you do things just because you want to be noticed? Would you do something good if nobody would ever find out about it? Do you do good things hoping someone will find out about it just so they can say, "Good job," to you?

All these things are forms of pride. I always thought pride was "oh, I am better than that person," but it's not just that. It is so much more. Pride comes in different forms. If you humble yourself, God will promote you. I want you to say this to people from now on when people complement you: "Everything you see here (you can even point to yourself) I cannot take credit for. It's all from God."

GOD IS MORE CONCERNED WITH WHAT MOTIVATES YOU TO DO SOMETHING, not what you did.

See No Evil:

The same concept about music goes with movies, T.V. shows, magazines, books, and whatever else your eyes can see.

Think about it for a second. Images are powerful. What we see and take in can stir/trigger emotions; we can know a place of business just from an image. Example: McDonalds, Nike, and BMW. Each of their symbols is recognized by people across the world, and they know what they stand for and what they can expect just by seeing that image/logo. A good advertiser knows its market, and they make commercials targeted to their audience. It's sad but true. At my former job as a gambling prevention specialist, I would educate people about the dangers of gambling. After a while, the state representatives wanted to make horse racing legal in my county. I was against this. I said that if we increase the availability of casinos and/or gambling, then we will create a new market for gamblers. They responded by saying in an article that the people who gamble on horses are older and will soon be passing away. But they needed a new race casino so they could advertise to a younger generation and keep off track betting alive. Basically, they admitted the need to advertise to the youth and how they would have to make things flashy, fast-paced, and eye-stimulating to entice young people's interest. The power of media is very important to understand.

This is one of the fourteen amendments that I still struggle with. Think about it. We as a society are seeing so much pain, death, rape, murder, theft, and violence in movies and video games that we are becoming numb in real life. Little kids are playing video games and watching movies with these themes. No wonder our society is so messed up. Before I go any further, I want you to list your top seven favorite movies or T.V. shows (I would prefer, if you don't mind, that you list movies).

1. ____________________
2. ____________________
3. ____________________
4. ____________________
5. ____________________
6. ____________________
7. ____________________

Now take a few minutes to really think of what each movie is about, as well as the language used, sexual content, violence, etc. Or maybe they are love stories. Consider whether they are realistic or not. Are they so fairytale-ish that they do not compare to your real relationship? Are the fake love stories causing you to compare your life with the character; thus you now feel less of a person and are in bondage from this? This step can and will set you free from these type of situations. Many, if not all of us, don't put much thought about what we watch. But trust me, God showed me this early on in my walk that we model after what we watch. We chase, assume the identity of, and compare our lives to the lives we are consuming our time with. This can trap us in pain, suffering, disappointment, and in some circumstances, a lifestyle that we never truly wanted. Remember my gangster/mafia craze I talked about? My point exactly! That is why it is so important that we visualize and speak the right things into our lives and into our family's life. Even to this day, as I write this, I still struggle with my flesh for this pastime because I truly enjoy those types of movies. One thing I like to do to relax is to sit down and watch a good gangster film—this brings enjoyment to me. But if I start watching too many of them, I notice that I start to slowly crave for that life style again—that way of talk, dress, actions. Same goes for drug dealing movies. I can watch one every now and then, but too often I start to think about money, drugs, that lifestyle, and it begins to look appealing to me again. This is something I have to be aware of. You may not be as bound by those images as I am or was, but the enemy is subtle, so we always have to be careful. Be vigilant. The Bible says give *no* place for the devil! I recommend that while you are reading this book and going through the amendments, you completely avoid certain types of music and movies that carry themes that "speak to" or stir you (you'll know which ones). Replace them with positive uplifting music and positive uplifting movies. Trust me, this will change your life forever. This is why it is so imperative to chase after God with our entire heart, be consumed by Him—this will set us free.

Scriptures

Psalm 101:3 ESV

I will not set before my eyes anything that is worthless. I hate the work of those who fall away; it shall not cling to me.

Philippians 4:8 ESV

Finally, brothers, whatever is true, whatever is honorable, whatever is just, whatever is pure, whatever is lovely, whatever is commendable, if there is any excellence, if there is anything worthy of praise, think about these things.

1 Corinthians 15:33 ESV

Do not be deceived: "Bad company ruins good morals."

Galatians 6:8 ESV

For the one who sows to his own flesh will from the flesh reap corruption, but the one who sows to the Spirit will from the Spirit reap eternal life.

Matthew 5:29 ESV

If your right eye causes you to sin, tear it out and throw it away. For it is better that you lose one of your members than that your whole body be thrown into hell.

1 Timothy 4:7 ESV

Have nothing to do with irreverent, silly myths. Rather train yourself for godliness;

Galatians 5:13 ESV

For you were called to freedom, brothers. Only do not use your freedom as an opportunity for the flesh, but through love serve one another.

Galatians 5:19-21 ESV

Now the works of the flesh are evident: sexual immorality, impurity, sensuality, idolatry, sorcery, enmity, strife, jealousy, fits of anger, rivalries, dissensions, divisions, envy, drunkenness, orgies, and things like these. I warn you, as I warned you before, that those who do such things will not inherit the kingdom of God.

James 4:4 ESV

You adulterous people! Do you not know that friendship with the world is enmity with God? Therefore whoever wishes to be a friend of the world makes himself an enemy of God.

Romans 12:2 ESV

Do not be conformed to this world, but be transformed by the renewal of your mind, that by testing you may discern what is the will of God, what is good and acceptable and perfect.

Romans 6:1–5

What shall we say then? Are we to continue in sin that grace may abound? By no means! How can we who died to sin still live in it? Do you not know that all of us who have been baptized into Christ Jesus were baptized into his death? We were buried therefore with him by baptism into death, in order that, just as Christ was raised from the dead by the glory of the Father, we too might walk in newness of life. For if we have been united with him in a death like his, we shall certainly be united with him in a resurrection like his.

Matthew 5:28 ESV

But I say to you that everyone who looks at a woman with lustful intent has already committed adultery with her in his heart.

Chapter Seven
Amendment 6 and Amendment 7

Spend Time with the Lord and Keep a Journal

The next two steps are shorter and similar to a workbook, so I am going to combine them into one chapter. The first step we will talk about is the importance of spending time with the Lord.

Amendment 6:

Spend Time with the Lord

Spending time with the Lord seems elementary, but throughout my ministry, time and time again, I have come across Christians who do not read the Bible regularly, do not pray regularly, and think that just one Sunday service qualifies as "spending time with the Lord." People look at it like a *chore* instead of something they WANT TO DO. I am honored to spend time with the Lord, because it is a privilege. We need to change our outlook. Think of the person you love most in this world. What do you want to do all the time? Love them, get to know them, talk to them, fellowship with them, or just being in their presence. If this is the case with humans in our lives, how much more should it be with Jesus, the one who was tortured, mocked, and murdered just for us? If you were the only one in this world, He would have come down from His throne and suffered for you, so you can have everlasting life. That is how much he loves you. He shows us this kind of love and the most we can give back is a few hours on a Sunday? Or a quick twenty-second prayer before we eat? Relationships do not work this way, my friends. Like someone you love, the more time you spend with them and the more you get to know them, the stronger that love is and the stronger that relationship is. And you become one—just like Jesus wants to become one with us through our relationship with him.

One way to get closer to God is through our prayer. Prayer is how we communicate with our God. Acts 6:4 says, "We will give ourselves continually to prayer and to the ministry of the word." This is powerful. Let's look at the word "continually." In Greek, "continually" is *proskartereó* (pros-kar-ter-eh'-o), which means to be earnest towards, to constantly adhere, continue, constant. This is how we are supposed to pray. Prayer builds our relationship with God. Philippians 4:6 says, "Do not be anxious about anything, but in every situation, by prayer and petition, with thanksgiving, present your requests to God. And the peace of God, which transcends all understanding, will guard your hearts and your minds in Christ Jesus." So in every situation in life, whether good or bad, the Bible tells us to pray, just pray. In Ephesians 6:18, the word of God says, "And pray in the spirit on ALL occasions with ALL kinds of prayers and request. With this in mind, be alert and always keep on praying for all the saints." The Amplified version says, "Pray at all times (on every occasion, in every season) in the spirit with all (manner of) prayer and entreaty. So we are supposed to pray at all times in every occasion, in every season." So when do we pray? **At all times.** In what? **In every occasion.** What then is an "occasion"? It's every season of our lives—at work, getting in a car, going on vacation, or in being tempted, being stressed, or looking for a job. In all things, we should pray. We usually share these things with a spouse or a close friend. God is telling you to share them with Him through prayer, just like you would share and communicate them with a loved one. If you thought you might be losing your job, or someone made you angry, you would talk it out, you would call someone. Think of God this way in your prayer. Reach out to Him, talk to Him, get to know Him, and trust Him.

You should out set time every day to pray to God. I have found that saying small breath prayers (see details below) throughout the day helps me build my relationship with Jesus. Not only am I communicating, but I'm yielding to Him, asking Him for help. I am thinking of Him more. Joyce Meyers said: "You and I live by breathing, our physical bodies require that we inhale and exhale, and the air sustains our bodies. In the same way, our spiritual lives are designed to be nurtured and sustained by PRAYER" (Amplified Study Bible).

Just like a boxer throws a 1-2-3-4 combo without even thinking, or how we breathe when we need to, we can pray this way at all times in every season on every occasion in every place. Jesus wants to be included in everything—activities, conversations, problems, and thoughts. This will not only build your relationship with Him, but will also create a bond that cannot be broken.

I am going to give you a few examples of my breath prayers. You can use mine, but I am also going to give you room to write your own. I encourage you to start using them twice a day for a week. Force yourself to remember to do it, and after a while, you will be filling up your entire day with breath prayers. In order to get closer to God, you just have to do two things: spend time with him and communicate with him. Amendment 6 is that simple! You do those two things and God will become more real to you than you can imagine.

Breath prayers:

- Jesus, you are with me.
- Jesus, give me wisdom.
- Thank you, Jesus, for your grace.
- I receive your grace and mercy.
- I belong to you, Jesus.
- I'm depending on you, Jesus.
- The glory of the Lord is upon me.
- I have favor every place I go.
- Doors are opening for me. Thank you, Jesus.

Now I want you to write your own breath prayers that you will use throughout your day:

____________________	____________________
____________________	____________________
____________________	____________________
____________________	____________________

Scriptures

Matthew 6:33 ESV

But seek first the kingdom of God and his righteousness, and all these things will be added to you.

Matthew 6:6 ESV

But when you pray, go into your room and shut the door and pray to your Father who is in secret. And your Father who sees in secret will reward you.

Romans 10:17 ESV

So faith comes from hearing, and hearing through the word of Christ.

1 Peter 2:2 ESV

Like newborn infants, long for the pure spiritual milk, that by it you may grow up into salvation.

Amendment 7:

Keep a Journal

Do you want to experience true freedom? If you want to be set free—I mean, truly set free from all those hidden secret feelings that have tortured you over the years—then pay attention. One of the most important things to do in life is keeping a journal. It will change your life. I tell this to people at churches I minister to, as well as worldly people I do presentations for. Journaling is for everyone. Write in your journal the people you have met, people you lost, your comings and goings, your triumphs, your impressions, your testimonies, your failures, or your disappointments—journal everything. A journal can also be a tool for self-evaluation and self-improvement. We can examine our lives as we come to know ourselves through our journals. A journal should show your true self, the self that nobody else sees. You can put down your false façade at the end of each day and let your real self out to talk, complain, cry, laugh; it is a safe place. This process will uncage feelings you did not even know you had, and then set you free from them.

Journaling also improves your health, reduces stress, and builds stronger relationships (writing about someone you know will help you understand them better). It also creates better organizational skills, awareness, and better focus. In addition, you can expect better solutions to problems (writing about problems gives your brain food for creative problem-solving), personal growth, and enhanced intuition. These are all benefits of keeping a journal. Not to mention you should write what you want to pray for, then record what God tells you. Now if you have a bad day and you journal about it, do not just leave the journal with negative feelings and turmoil. End your journal entry with positives. End it with what God says about you or your situation. Write about what you hope to do the next day and the things you hope to change.

Scripture

Numbers 33:2

At the Lord's direction, Moses kept a written record of their progress. These are the stages of their march, identified by the different places where they stopped along the way.

Chapter Eight
Amendment 8

Image and Mind-Set

Your mind-set creates your image; it molds your life. Your image helps develop your character, and your character defines who you are as a person. Therefore, you can see why this step is so important. Your mind-set determines who you are, where you are going, and how you are going to get there. Almost all of the choices you make in life are intertwined with your image. Your image is so powerful that it fuels your life; it produces your consequences. I say this because most of us will make choices based upon who we think we are or how we see ourselves. Understand that we are free to choose whatever we want in life, but we are not free to choose our consequences. Those come from our choices. Where you are right now is a result of decisions you made or did not make in your past. Even if something negative (that you couldn't control) occurred in your past, you still had the ability to choose your *response* to that event. So consequently, your current self is still based upon a decision that you made. And where you are five years from now will be a result of the choices you are presently making. We often live by how we feel. If we want something badly enough, then we are willing to do whatever it takes to get it. Sin then is produced when our choices/actions are derived from a lack of trust in God to meet certain things in our lives, including our needs and feelings. As a result of these poor, godless decisions, we create pain from our need to react. This need is fueled from childhood hurts and a misguided self-image. We then mask our pain with sin. Sin becomes the Tylenol®, the pain reliever. When we try to change our own strength, we focus on our sin, not the root cause of it—our pain. Our real focus should be on overcoming our identity. The image that screams "I am worthless, I am a loser, I am different than everyone else." This all comes from our hurt—the part of ourselves that hasn't been turned over to God. Even if you believe that you had an ideal childhood, take a moment and create a virtual timeline. Consider the events of your life, both positive and negative, during your development years. List as much as you can remember for the ages 0–6, 6–10, 10–19, and 19 beyond.

0–6

____

____

____

6–10

____

____

____

10–19

____

____

____

19 plus

____

____

____

Do any events stick out? Can you identify a person or an experience that to this day causes a little bit of hurt, resentment, or lingering uneasiness? Did any of these events cause you to feel a particular way about yourself? For some, it may be one distinct event; for others, it may have several. I promise you, every time I've done this exercise, people always find their "pain point"—one specific event that they have forgotten but subconsciously lingered through adulthood and has essentially shaped the image of who they are today. This pain point of what had happened now causes a feeling inside them that they cover up with a sinful act. One man who did this exercise began to remember that his parents always made him go outside every day so they could have personal time together. They would say to him, "We want to be alone. You need to go outside and find some friends and play." This seeming innocent situation made him feel rejected by his parents and not wanted. This feeling lately crept into his marriage and eventually began to destroy it, because he did not think he was worthy enough to be loved. Deep down, he felt worthless and unwanted. This was his image of himself. To be restored, this man needs to be introduced to the image God had created for him and learn to see himself for who really is.

As we have been doing, I will first define "image," share personal examples, and then finally provide scriptural references.

Let me start off by asking you to think about this next question. I want you to close your eyes and think for as long as it takes until you have a vivid picture in your mind. Do you have an image—the way people see you and the way you see yourself? And what is that image? Now close your eyes for a few minutes and think about those questions.

Write down your image here:

____

____

____

Now ask yourself, "Where has that image gotten me?"

____

____

____

The image we carry can be positive or negative, uplifting of defeating. Sadly, for many Christians, their self-image greatly contrasts with who God says we are and how *He* sees us. This can cause people to feel hopeless because they feel like they don't belong. So how are these images formed? Self-image is how you perceive yourself; it is a number of self-impressions that have been built up over time. Your self-image determines your hopes and dreams, what you think and feel. Do you see yourself as hopeless, a drunk, a loser, angry, unworthy, a druggie, a thug, or better than everyone else? Image is something parents give to their children. If your parents give you a low self-worth, you can and will grow up feeling worthless. An image can control your life.

Remember my dad? I talked about him a lot in chapter one. His anger became my image; I became angry. We look up to our fathers. We mimic them, learn from them, and create our own image from them. If they are unhealthy, chances are we will be, too. I became a slave to anger. I had no respect for adults so I would act out. I remember one year when my tenth-grade teacher told me in front of the entire class that I would end up in jail or dead by age twenty-five. That same year, my principal called me down to his office and yelled, "You are worthless and do not belong in my school. I think you should drop out. Why can't you be more like your brother?" These words (we talked about the power of words) molded my image (caused a lot of pain in my life years later). I saw myself as an angry tough kid who was worthless and dumb. Someone nobody really wanted around and had no future. Having no future or worth led to many of my bad choices, including using and selling drugs. I had nothing to lose; I was already worthless. We talked about the power of music and movies. Well, that is where I turned to find myself a new image. The direction you set your mind towards is the direction that your life will be pulled towards. My mom, grandmother, and aunt all deposited positive self-images into my life, but I was so bombarded by negative ones that I never noticed the positive voices that were also there. Now, looking back, I can see the work they did, and I am so thankful for the seeds they planted in me. *(Sometimes seeds take a long time to grow. A person can change at any time, but all change takes time.)*

I will ask you again, what is the image you have of yourself? Now start thinking how you have lived your life around this image. After my dad left, I gravitated towards the images I saw on TV and music. I witnessed behaviors from older guys whom everyone feared. And I wanted to be feared. Why? My dad made me feel helpless, so I wanted this image of a gangster that nobody could push around, so nobody could hurt me again. I never wanted to feel helpless again. I mimicked these actors and musicians. I talked like them, dressed like them, swore like them, sold drugs like them, robbed liked them, stole and fought like them. They weren't even real. They were selling an image to make money, and I was so lost that I was buying it. It became my reality. Fast-forward and after decades of being the "tough" guy, I met Christ and gave Him my life and my image. Here comes the turning point. You believe in God and all that He has done, but you still hold on to the "old" image. This creates a separation, a feeling of being alone, an outcast, and a feeling of hopelessness. You start coming to church miserable.

You don't fit in, and no matter what you do, you cannot feel happy. You feel this way because your old image is fighting with your new image. Even if you are not acting on the old image and you are walking with God, it is still in your mind.

Mind-Set

This is how you look at things in life. My darkest season in life started when I was away in college. I was doing well, wasn't drinking, and wasn't selling drugs. I was honoring the promise I'd made my mother (see chapter one). She was so proud of me that she would brag about me any chance she had. I would drive home on the weekends to surprise her, and sometimes even on a weekday just to take her out to dinner. I loved my mom, and I'd sworn to protect her no matter what. One day I got a phone call. I remember I was in my dorm room. The door was open. People were in the halls talking and yelling. People were in my room talking. Chaos was all around, but the good kind. Suddenly, everything went black and all noises ceased. I heard nothing except, "They found small amounts of cancer, honey. I have to get an operation, but everything is going to be OK." That's all I remember. I don't remember what I said and what she said after that, nor do I remember what happened to all the people in my room or in the halls. Everything is a blur.

Nevertheless, I remember getting into my car and trying to drive home through the tears that were covering my eyes. I was crying out to God to have mercy on my mom, to save her. I told Him she was all I had and I could not live without her. I began to beg God to allow me to change places with her. I told Him, "Let me go through this. Take my life if you want to. Just leave my mom alone." Finally after what felt like hours in the car, I got home. I spent time with my mom. We talked, laughed, held each other, and cried. She told me one thing that to this day echoes through my mind.

She said, "Honey, whenever you are by my side, I feel like nothing bad can happen to me. I feel like you are my protector."

I told her, "Mom, I would burn down an entire city to protect you. I promise you that nothing will ever hurt you."

A few days later, she went into the operating room. Hours later, the doctor came out and walked over. In my mind, I was thinking, *"She said it was 'only a little.' They are going to remove it, and she would be fine."* So when the doctor opened his mouth and said that she had a ten-percent chance of recovering from surgery and that if she did recover, the percentage of her living much longer was very low. My world came crashing down. I could not hear, see, or talk. I just walked out of the hospital. I felt so angry, but there was nothing to be angry at. I felt helpless and scared. I had no idea what to do. My family and I went to tell my grandmother the news (her mother). When she heard it, she let out a scream that would bring any person to their knees. So many things happened so quickly that to this day, I cannot remember all that happened. No details. My mom recovered from the surgery. People prayed for her. People were telling me that she was going to be healed and that God had a plan for her. They told me not to worry; everything was going to be all right. I took this at face value and believed. My mom was going to be fine. She would be healed because I could not live without her, and God knew this.

This is where things start to get blurry. Basically, my mom started to go through chemotherapy. Then my grandma (her mom) got sick and it was found out to be cancer. She got an operation and was supposed to be fine. The doctors actually said, "We got it all; she will recover and be fine." But life didn't work out that way. My mother's cancer went into remission. Shortly after, my grandmother died. Then the Twin Towers were destroyed by terrorists on 9/11, the same day my mother's cancer returned. I remembered friends at college panicking because they were from New York; they had family there. I could not focus; it seemed like death, destruction, and chaos were in every place I looked on that day.

"This can't be, God! What is going on?" I remembered begging God, "Please, take me and not my mom. Just heal her, I will do anything; I will give you my life."

I watched my mom suffer like no human should have in a hospital bed for months. She couldn't talk, move, or go to the bathroom. She had blood clots and lungs filled with fluid. Once during a blood transfusion, her arm began to swell up like a balloon. I screamed for help; nobody came. I yelled as she held my hand, saying, "Don't leave me." And I still believed she was going to be healed because everyone told me she would be.

A few weeks before college graduation, my mom got enough strength to talk. "Colby, I love you so much. Do you know heaven is just right around the corner? It's like a block away, just around the corner. And if I go there, I am not in your past. I will be in your future. Let me go, Colby. I want to go home."

I kissed her and told her I love her more than I love anything in this world; I would die for her. I then said, "Go home, Mom. Go home." I was crying and was hurting so much because I realized I could not protect her, and I was supposed to be her protector. There was nothing I could do to change this. I was completely helpless. The next morning, St. Patrick's Day, March 17, 2002, she went home to be with the Lord. She never got to see me graduate from college. I remembered my aunt (her sister) coming up after me and saying, "I am your mom now. I will be here for you, baby. I love you." Those are the memories I have, all this.

Afterwards, I completely turned my back on God; I walked away from him and his church. A short time after graduation from college, I had no place to live. I had to stay at my older brother's house while he and his wife were expecting their first child. I had no job, nor much money. I was all alone, and I came to the conclusion that nobody in this world will ever help you out, so you need to do whatever you can to make it. At this time, my mind-set was that God didn't care for me. I'd asked him to heal my mom, and he didn't. God didn't answer my prayers because he didn't really love me. My mind-set was a mess. Before I tell you how it changed, let's go back to self-image for a minute.

Reprograming Your Image

The Bible says in Romans 12:2, "Do not be conformed to this world." Basically, it is saying do not get your image from things of this world. It goes on to say, "... but be transformed by the renewal of your mind." In Greek, "transformed" means *metamorphoó* (met-am-or-fo'-o), which is the root word for "metamorphosis," to change, transfigure. "Renewing" means make new, relearning, reprogramming. Basically, it's telling you to dump the hard drive of your mind with thoughts of who you think you are and reprogram yourself. You ask, "What will you reprogram your brain to?" You will reprogram your brain to the world of God. You will read what He says about you and how He sees you. And the word of God is saying that you are His child. So reprogram yourself as a child of God. 1 John 3:1: "See what kind of love the Father has given to us, that we should be called children of God: and so we are." Look at this. We are children of God. This is who we *really* are, our real image. Because of God's love, I am a child of His. If I am a child of His, then I am not worthless, dumb, retarded, a thug, a slave to anger, or a drug dealer. I am wearing a new image now. You, too, need to reprogram your thoughts and your brain to the "I am a child of God" thinking. You are righteous and royal; you are a son/daughter of God. Start to say this out loud as many times a day as you can. This is how you rehabilitate your image. If you do not want to say it out loud, at least write it down; otherwise, it will never translate into reality. If you can visualize your relationship to God and truly accept it, your pain will lessen. You will stop focusing on trying to "be" good, because you are already good in God's eyes. You are righteous in His eyes, complete, finished. Image is often the primary way the enemy tries to attacks us. Think about it. Why did Eve eat the apple? The devil put it in her head that she was incomplete, lacking something, and that she needed something else to become better. So she gave into temptation because the enemy attacked her image. When you start to live with a new image, people in the world will not be able to relate to you because your action will be different from theirs. They will start to say, "What you mean you do not drink, go to bars, swear, or sleep around? That does not make sense to us." You will find that friends and family will try to bring you down. But let's continue with 1 John 3:1. "The reason why the world does not know you is that it did not know me." 1 John 3:3 says, "He is pure if you hope in Jesus." Therefore, if you are pure, then you are no longer a slave to sin, anger, drugs, and so on. Say this out loud: "I am pure. This is my image. I am a child of God. I am pure." Pure means free from anything that adulterates, taints; blameless, absolute, faultless.

Write this verse out and read it at least once a day: "I am the righteousness of God through faith in Jesus Christ for all who believe. For there is no distinction," (Romans 3:22).

____

____

Write, "I am pure because I am a child of God." Then read it out loud every day.

____

____

Earlier I talked about how, as a child, we look to our parents as role models to get our image. The Bible tells us in Ephesians 5:1, "Be followers of God as DEAR CHILDREN." Children look up to their parents. The offsprings study their father and mother; they watch their parents when no one else is watching them. So we are supposed to do this with God. Since He is our Father and our new image is as His child, we are supposed to imitate Him and model our lives after Him. By reading your Bible, you are getting to know

God on a personal level. Also, you can learn from the people who have been walking with God for a long time in your church. As they walk, walk with them.

Mind-Set

Changing your mind-set can be difficult, but you can do it. A positive mind anticipates happiness, joy, health, and successful future. This is what God told me: "You have to first be thankful for what you have instead of complaining about what you don't have." Thank God for everything in your life. Look at things that happen in life as opportunities to grow. When things do not go your way, do not get mad and blame God. Instead, thank the Lord and say, "Thank you for this opportunity to learn something new." Speak blessings into each circumstance instead of panic and negativity. Get rid of all negative thoughts.

Whatever the mind expects, it finds. If you expect pain, defeat, or failure, then your mind will find it. You need to visualize and expect positive images. I use this same principle when I talk to the youth. I tell them, "You need to visualize yourself making a good impression at a job interview. You need to visualize yourself getting the job." So how does visualizing change your mind-set? When we visualize what we want to happen, we start to feel happy and we get more energy. It will bring brightness to our eyes, and our voice starts to sound more powerful and confident. I have spent a good portion of my life studying body language. I can tell whether a certain person is positive or negative. Our body language shows the way we feel. So if we sit up, smile, walk taller, or make eye contact—things like that—it shows that we are confident and positive. Positive and negative thinking are contagious. We want to be around positive people. I do not know anyone who actually enjoys the company of negative people—those who are always complaining and looking at the worst case in every situation. We tend to avoid negative people like we avoid people with the flue. Positive thoughts bring positive feelings that fill our hearts and bring forth positive words. Negative thoughts bring negative feelings that discourage our hearts and bring forth negative words. This leads to unhappy moods and actions.

Whatever you fill your mind with, your life will eventually be filled with. Thoughts become imagination. Before you know it, you are always thinking and meditating on these thoughts that then become a strong hold (almost like an addiction, a way of life, a belief) in your life. This goes for positive and negative thoughts. If you always think of the worst, your body is always tense. It is automatically prepared for two things: fight or flight. You will either be ready to knuckle up and fight or lace up your shoes and run, avoiding the problem. I have learned the hard way in life that we as humans love to avoid things based on fear. Fear is something that has not happened yet; we do not fear things that have already happened. I am not losing sleep and worrying about the doctor's appointment I had last week because I already had it. Now I may be worrying about the test results that I have not gotten yet. If we allow fear in our hearts, our imaginations/thoughts will wage war on us. Instead of meditating/thinking about positive things and what God says about us, we sometimes allow our thoughts to give us a death sentence. I once heard that thoughts, whether good or bad, create chemical pathways in your brain that form patterns (in thoughts and behavior). This is why we contently think of the same negative or positive thing when the same type of incident occurs over and over again in our life.

So what can be done? When your mind is rewired, peace will be there. Stop using your past experiences as the administrator of your future. Remove the walls and barriers of your thinking. Use your imagination to visualize and encourage yourself in each situation. You need to smile a little more because this will help you think positively and say positive words. This is hard but you have to become intentional on what you think about—it means get rid of all negative thoughts. You have to realize that our brains are always thinking about our past situations that has molded who we are today. We have to break those thought patterns by intentionally interrupting them and focusing on something else positive. Think of your mind like a television screen. Every time a negative thought comes into the picture, you need to change the channel, do something else, think differently, or call a friend. In some cases, you may even have to rearrange a room—your bedroom, living room, or what have you—to create a new image of the place in your mind. For example, when you lie down to sleep, that is when negative thoughts come into your head. So now that space in your mind is associated with negativity. Even if you do not know it, your mind sees that room and automatically starts to have thoughts of worry and negativity. So what you need to do is move the elements in your room around. Start visualizing positive things in that room. Try to laugh and remember happy thoughts. Soon that space will be associated with new images; you will have created a different mind-set.

Once you start this process, your mind will change forever. Every great building was built because someone imagined it, thought about it, visualized it. It started in their mind. Please pay attention to the next statement I will make. Write it down if you have to. You cannot change a single thing that has happened in the past. It's locked in, done; you can't undo it. However, from this very moment forward, you can write and mold your own destiny.

There are many things you cannot control in life. You cannot control people's perception of you, what they say about you, how you are treated. There's so much more in this life that we cannot control, but you can control how you react to the things you cannot control. You can control the way you think, what you think about, what you meditate on, and what you confess out of your mouth. You need a new mind-set, an imagination, and the ability to see a vision that nobody else can see. This will give you a new life. Are you willing to break down the walls of your brain? Are you willing to smash through your limited imagination, your vision, and your negative thought patterns? This is the only way you can change the behaviors you've been struggling with for years. No, it's not by white knuckling your way through them or through temptations. Try to think of something else. Change your thoughts. Think about Jesus. If you suffer from depression every time a bad thought comes into your brain, think of something you are grateful for. Call a friend or think of what Jesus has done for you. After a while, your brain will be reprogramed.

The loss of my mom almost destroyed me. Then I began to use this same amendment and started to look at her loss differently. I remembered all the positive moments we shared together. I stopped looking at it as a loss and started to realize that she was not in my past; rather, I would see her again in my future. I looked at the positives of heaven, being with Jesus. Instead of feeling hurt that she was gone, I feel excited for the new life she was living now, how happy she is, and how peaceful she is. Thinking of these things brings a smile to my face. For the first time, my eyes became open. My mom no longer feels any pain; nothing will ever disappoint her again. She will never be scared again. Tears of joy fill my eyes at her happy scenario. I used to look at myself as her protector. For years, I blamed myself for allowing her to die when I told her she could go home. I felt like I failure. But now I realize that by letting her go, she is able to be with the ultimate protector; nothing can ever hurt her again. I protected her by letting her go, and just like my mom said before she left, "Dear, don't worry. I am just right around the corner. I will see you soon, baby." I am in great joy now knowing that she is safe, happy, and waiting for me.

I told you earlier that my aunt stepped in to be my new "mom." So when I walked away from God after my mother passed, my aunt stood by my side and was always there for me. No matter what I did in life, she would tell me what the word of God said about it and then just love me. As a matter of fact, I learned all about God's love through my aunt because she was a walking example of it. I was in a hospital one day for chest pains. I thought I was having a heart attack. My aunt stayed with me the entire time, holding my hand, smiling, and telling me that everything was going to be "OK." When she told me everything was going to be OK, it was like God himself was saying it. I was filled with peace and joy. All the tests came back fine, just like she'd said. A few years later, when I had another health problem, she said to me, "Baby, do not worry. No matter what happens, I will be by your side every step of the way." It wasn't the words she spoke that brought comfort; it was the love entangled with her words.

Years after, in answer to God's incessant calls, I finally chose to come back (free will can destroy us) to the church. This time it felt different. I started to realize who Jesus really is and how much he loves me. This time was for keeps and I knew it. I became a member at my local church and started to go to service with my brother, sister-in-law, and aunt. We would go out to breakfast after service and just fellowship. This would fill me with joy and love. After about a year, I got baptized. Shortly after that, I found out that my aunt has only a few weeks to live. It seemed to happen just that fast. It felt like I got dunked in water and now was looking at another death in the family, my last "Mom." She fought for a few weeks and finally said to me, "It is what it is. I am ready to go home."

Then it was like someone pushed "pause," and I was looking at another life-changing moment. God gave me the opportunity to use this amendment in a very real and practical way. I could either run away again and blame God or hold onto God, look at the positive, and just ride it out. I picked number two. I told God, "I am staying with you, Lord, no matter what. You can't get rid of me." I looked at my aunt and told her, "I do not blame you, Aunt Holly. Go home, get out of here, and say 'hi' to our family when you get there." I said this with a big smile, and then I hugged her. I was sad. I went through sorrow. I grieved. But this time I went back to serving the Lord. I changed my mind-set and looked at the positives. This step kept me going, kept me serving the Lord, and kept me remembering the good times my aunt and I had together, knowing

I will see her and my mom again. The same day my aunt passed away was the same day I got fired from my job, found out that my phone was wired for two years, and was looking at possible prison time. Without the power of Jesus, I could not have made it through and beyond that day. I would have more setbacks, like the period that prompted the letter I wrote in chapter three, but because my mind-set had changed regardless of the knockdowns—and there would be many—I continued to get back up and fight (after all, my mom raised me to be a fighter). With God on my side, all things are possible.

Activity

The activity in this section has just one exercise, but it will take you a month to complete. For the next thirty days, when you wake up, list ten things for which you are grateful. At first, you will think this is too difficult. But as you force your mind to be positive, it will become easier. I want you to say it out loud when you write it. You can say, "Thank you, God, for I can breathe. Thank you, God, for you woke me up today. Thank you, God, for my job. Thank you, God, for the green grass I see out of my window today. Thank you, God, for my brother. Thank you, God, for my church"—and/or whatever else there may be. You don't have to write complete sentences; a word or two is fine. But I suggest you read it out loud as if it were a sentence.

For example:

Write: Mom
Say: I am thankful that I had such a loving and forgiving mother.

Complete the first week using the space below. On the next three weeks, get a notebook and use that.

Monday:__________

Tuesday:__________

Wednesday:__________

Thursday:__________

Friday:__________

Saturday:__________

Sunday:__________

Scriptures

Colossians 3:2

And set your minds and keep them set on what is above (the higher things) not on the things that are on the earth.

- Basically saying see things how Jesus sees them, don't see things how the world sees it. Your mind needs to picture life how Jesus does.

Proverbs 4:23

Keep and guard your heart with all vigilance and above all that you guard, for out of it flows the springs of life.

Matthew 15:18

But the things that come out of the mouth come from the heart and mind, and these make a man "unclean."

Matthew 15:19

For out of the heart comes evil thoughts (reasoning and disputing and designs) such as murder, adultery, sexual vice, theft, false witnessing, slander and irreverent speech.

A Few Scriptures about the Image of God in which We Are Created

Say these out loud as you read them.

I am complete in Him who is the head of all principality and power (Colossians 2:10).

I am alive with Christ (Ephesians 2:5).

I am free from the law of sin and death (Romans 8:2).

I am born of God, and the evil one does not touch me (1John 5:18).

I have the peace of God that surpasses all understanding (Philippians 4:7).

I am more than a conqueror through him who loves me (Roman 8:37).

I am an ambassador for Christ (2 Corinthians 5:20).

I am redeemed from the curse of sin, sickness, and poverty (Deuteronomy 28:15–68 and Galatians 3:13).

Chapter Nine
Amendment 9

Choices, Vision, Purpose

This chapter will deal about the three main things involved in the process of changing your life. Here we will talk about (1) choices, how to make choices and how choices can keep you on or off track with your purpose; (2) vision, finding a vision through goals and how to make short and long-term goals (your vision gives you hope, and hope is what creates change; hope is what Jesus gives each and every one of us. [For example, for this book I had a vision: **To give hope to the hopeless and to inspire people who love God but haven't been able to truly tap into HIS love**]); and (3) purpose, how to find your purpose in life, which is the reason God put you on this earth in this particular time.

What if I blindfold you, put you in my car, and drive around aimlessly. After a while I will pull over, get out of the car, and walk over to your door. All you hear are my footsteps, and then the door opens. As I open the door, I say, "Stand up, leave the blindfold on, and try to find your way home." Then I will drive off. How difficult do you think it would be to find your way home while walking blindfolded and with no idea where you are? What will happen?

Well, you will try, but chances are you will not make it home. You will eventually give up and take the blindfold off to get a vision.

This is a lot like life. If we do not have a vision of where we *want* to go, then we have no idea where *we are going*. If we have no goal or purpose, we are going to walk aimlessly until we come to the end of our life and say, "Wow, how did I end up here? Oh, that's right! I had no vision. I just walked from job to job, relationship to relationship, until I got tired of walking and gave up."

Choices

In my entire life, I just did what I wanted to do and when I wanted to do it. I never had goals, never had a purpose, and never thought about my choices. And now, when I go out and speak to the youth and adults throughout the community, I basically hear the same thing.

I will ask, "How did you get here?"

They will answer, "I don't know. It just happened."

Then I will go deeper and say, "Did you plan on being here? Being this way?"

They'll then reply, "I never really thought about it."

I want you to take a second and think of your life and how many times you never thought of your choices and where they'd lead. How many times have you gone with the crowd because it seemed like the right thing or the fun thing to do? Without a vision, we walk aimlessly through life with no purpose.

This is so alarming to me because I lived the majority of my life the same way. Then I said to myself, "How the heck did I get here? What happened?" This chapter will help you change that. If done correctly, this amendment will be a step-by-step blueprint into your God-focused future. Perhaps, for the first time in years, you will feel like you actually matter, that you have a reason to be here on earth, that God wants to use you for His plan.

First, let's talk about the choices we make in everyday life. To get started, we'll do a quick exercise. In the space provided, I want you to write down all the "choices" you made yesterday. Take your time and think about it.

Choices I Made:

_______________ _______________
_______________ _______________
_______________ _______________
_______________ _______________
_______________ _______________
_______________ _______________
_______________ _______________
_______________ _______________
_______________ _______________
_______________ _______________
_______________ _______________
_______________ _______________

If you really thought about this, there should not be enough room to write down all the choices you made in a day. Like I said, we have become so complacent in our decision making that choices are forgotten. For example, your morning decisions might look like this: Time you decided to get out of bed—to hit the snooze or not, to go to the bathroom or make coffee first, to eat breakfast or not, if so what breakfast? To shave or not to shave? Read the Bible or just pray—what to pray? What Bible verse to read? What to wear to work—dress up or casual? What socks? What type of underwear? Does this match? Do I look fat wearing this? Should I change into this? Do I bring a lunch or buy a lunch? I could keep on going and that was just an example of the morning of the entire day of choices I asked you to list.

One of my favorite scriptures is **Romans 6:16 (NLT)**. "Whatever you choose to obey becomes your master. You can choose sin which leads to death or you can choose to obey God that leads to everlasting life."

True power is the fact that we can make a choice, any choice, good or bad. Choice is the most sought-after desire from all humans. You can become a slave to your choices. Your choices can bring life or death.

How Many Times Have You Heard?

- If I were rich, I could choose to do whatever I want to do with my time.

I learned in Marketing 101 that the power of choice is what makes a company succeed. Giving people the choice in how they interact with your company is the basic rule in having a successful company. You are giving your customers the power to make the choices that suit them and not just offering what suits you.

Example:

- Have it your way right away. You choose how you want your food.
- You choose the clothing you want in a store.
- In shopping for a car, you choose the style, color, and seats.

How many of us are waiting, or have waited, for God to pick us up and throw us into our destiny? Well, I am very sad to smack you across the face, but God does not work that way. I once had this theory that God would just physically move me into my destiny. This theory did not work. You have to choose to walk with God so he can open doors to our calling and destiny. Then you have to choose to walk through them. People really take for granted the power of their choices. Just about every outcome in our lives can be traced back to a moment where *we* had a choice. That being said, we should really meditate and seek God before making a choice, no matter how small or insignificant the decision may seem.

We react to situations and feelings, and that determines our choice. The devil loves this. If he can get me to act without thinking or get me to "just react' to a situation, then nine out of ten times, I'll react in the flesh and end up sinning. In my life, I have come to realize that the less time I have to meditate and seek God on a choice in my life, the happier the devil is because he knows I will lean towards my flesh and my old way of life. We make a choice to allow ourselves to get mad or not. We choose to sin or not to sin.

What we take for granted many people have learned to cherish. People in prison lose many of their choices; that is why prison is such a hard place. Ask any inmate (I know many and have asked them) and they will tell you that the worst part of prison life is the lack of freedom of choice. You can no longer choose when to eat, when to get up, when to go to bed, when to shower. People choose them for you.

The Word says we were chosen by God, but we still have to choose to accept Christ into our hearts. That is why it is important to consider God in our choices and meditate on it before making any decision. Your choices ultimately determine the type of person you are and who you'll continue to be. So why not take each choice as a life or death matter?

Example:

You are driving in your car to a nearby store. It's your son's birthday, and you forgot the soda. You got less than fifteen minutes before the start of the party, so you are in a hurry. Then someone cuts you off and proceeds to give you the middle finger. You beep the horn and give the middle finger back. You grow upset and curse under your breath. Your heart begins to race, and your blood pressure keeps going up.

Let's take it a step further. He pulls over, so you pull up behind him. He gets out; you get out. Words are exchanged. Next thing you know, he is throwing a punch and you are punching back. You both are on the ground wrestling as your pastor and some of your church members drive by, waving and pointing. (Hey, look, honey! Isn't that Timmy's youth pastor rolling around on the ground with that man?)

The police show up. As you are being arrested, you think to yourself, "Where did I go wrong? What happened here? When did I lose control?" Your son is at home crying because Daddy is nowhere to be found.

We can continue building this scenario. You were arrested. Your name is now tarnished. Your boss is notified. He calls you into his office and fires you. You've just lost your job because he doesn't want a loose cannon who cannot control his anger in his office. Don't think this is too farfetched; it happens more than you know. Some people are clueless when these types of events occur. They ask questions: Why would God allow me to get fired? Why are things like this always happening to me? Why does God put me through so many trials?

That's why we cannot make our choices halfheartedly. We need to pray and ask the Holy Spirit for advice on what to do. If we make a choice in our flesh, we will choose worldly desires most of the time, and the Bible warns us against that. In 1 Peter 2:11, it says: "Dear friends, I warn you as temporary residents to keep away from worldly desires that wage war against your very soul. Be careful to live properly among your unbelieving neighbors."

Life is a series of choices. In order to be set free from pain and sin, we have to CHOOSE to let go. We have to CHOOSE to let God in and take over our lives. We have to CHOOSE to surrender everything to him and say, "Lord, my desires are dead now. Use me. Fill me with your desires. Direct my life." You can CHOOSE to move forward, AND you can CHOOSE to get back up and fight again. You will not do it in your own strength; God will do it for you. BUT you have to make a CHOICE. Remember when I told you I was going to lose my job? I chose not to be worried. I knew God had it under control; He told me. So, how do you make the right choice?

Helpful Hints:

- We constantly need to monitor where we are on our journey.
- Ask, "Am I moving closer to my goals or further?"

1) Start with the Beginning in Mind:

Look ahead and see how the choice you are about to make will shape your future. Someday we will live in the results of every choice we make now. In life, just like in choices, you need to know where you are going. If you look to the end of each choice, you will determine where you are going. Not every choice is a moral choice. Some are just smart choices and bad choices.

2) Positive Mind-Set:

Remember, we are certain to find what we are looking for. By thinking positive and setting positive goals, we will find positive outcomes. Believe that something good can happen in your life, no matter what you are going through right now. Choose to live with hope rather than live like you are already defeated.

3) Circumstances versus Self-Impressions:

In life, sometimes our circumstances are out of our control. No matter what we do or how we think, bad things happen, leaving us in a bad circumstance. Have the right attitude on how we view the trials we are facing. First, view them as challenges instead of problems. Choose to be positive and meditate on the positive we have. For example, I know a man with one leg. One day he got out of his car to help another person out, and he got hit by a car. He lost his leg as a result. Now he has a choice: he can either sit around thinking of the thousand things he could do with both legs or he can think of the 900 things he can still do without one leg.

4) Habits:

In life, we act out of habit rather than thinking through a choice. Then we end up in a rut or in the wrong place in life. We have to be intentional on our thinking pattern before making a choice. We need to always be looking for different opportunities that break us out of our normal habits. If you always act a certain way when something happens, and that is the thing you are trying to change, you must stop yourself and think in a different way so that your way of thinking becomes your habit. For example, every time someone disagrees with you or tries to correct you, you snap at them, you attack their character, and you tell them what you think is wrong with them. It is just a habit; it happens without thinking. Or every time you become stressed, you take drugs or drink alcohol to calm down and relax. It is just a habit; you do it without thinking. It is what you have always done. To break those habits, you need to stop before you act and say to yourself, "I am stressed. What can I do instead of drinking?" Or, "Someone is correcting me. OK, what can I learn from this?" Then after you break that thought pattern and create a new one, that habit will no longer be there. Remember to interrupt your thinking pattern before making a choice.

5) Break It Down Five Times:

a. The "5 Whys" is a problem-solving technique invented by the founder of Toyota. When something goes wrong, you ask why five times. By asking why something failed over and over, you eventually get to the root of the cause.
b. Although initially developed as a problem-solving technique, I used this concept with the youth all the time

to determine whether a choice you're considering is in line with your core values (your goals).

i. "Why should I take this job? It pays well and offers me a chance to grow. Why is that important? Because I want to build a career and not just have a string of meaningless jobs. Why? Because I want my life to have meaning. Why? So I can be happy. Why? Because that's what is important in life.

ii. Notice that sometimes you have to change how you ask why to keep the question focused inward rather than outward.

To Have a Future We Must Have Goals and Know Where We Are Going

Vision

Now that we talked about choices, we must talk about goals (vision). In order to continually make the right choices, you need to have a vision or a goal that you are working towards. My definition of "vision" in this book is this: "To see what is not there. To see and believe what no one else can; to see what you cannot view with your natural eyes."

If I hold up a stone and ask you what you see, most of you will say, "A stone." (I used this as a visual at a commencement speech I gave once.) A person with vision will say, "A castle," "A church," or "A cathedral." They have a vision and see something great in that stone. They see what nobody else sees—what could be there, not what is there.

A research I have done, after interacting over the years with youth, has shown that most teenagers do not have goals. And if they do, it is simply one or two (e.g., graduate and then go to college). I tell people all the time that the more specific they are with their goals, the clearer their vision will be, which will help them accomplish that goal.

Most people, on hearing the phrase "goal setting," will start to think about their future, job, and family.

1) It is necessary to set short-term goals—goals that can be reached in a day or a week.

Close your eyes and think of something you want to accomplish in the next week.

a. Visualize how you are going to accomplish it.
b. See the time frame in which you will accomplish it.

Activity

Write down the short-term goal you just visualized. Be specific. Share below how you visualized completing it and the time frame you gave yourself to accomplish it.

____

____

____

____

____

Assignment

After you accomplished this goal, come back to this chapter and write the date you have achieved it on the line below.

Date Accomplished: ________________

Helpful Hints for Goal Setting

- **Specific Goals:**
  - The more specific you are while making your goal, the more likely you will succeed at that goal. For example: I am going to lose 50 pounds this year. That is a very unspecific goal. So most likely, you will not accomplish that goal.
    - Improved version of goal:
      - I am going to wake up three times a week—Monday, Thursday, and Saturday—at 6:00 a.m. and jog three miles before work for the next year and stop eating fast food.

Now you have a goal with specific details on how you are going to reach that goal.

- **All Change Takes Time and Produces Character:**
  - Habits become character; our character becomes our destiny.
    - It means that everything I do in my day-to-day life makes up who I am (my character). Who I am and how I see myself will determine where I am going in life. That is my destiny.
    - Changing your habits takes a long time because you do it without thinking. So my habit is sleeping in till 11:00 a.m. every day. I want to start a new habit of getting up early to go to the gym. It will take a few months of getting up early before it becomes a habit and becomes easy. After a few months, it becomes a part of my daily routine; it will be a part of my life.
    - I have heard in a sermon from Pastor John Carter of Syracuse, New York, that it takes twenty-one (21) days to develop a new habit.

- **Repeating a Goal Makes It Stick:**

Say your goal out loud each morning to remind yourself of what you want and what you're working for. Write it down. Every time you remind yourself of your goal, you are training your brain to make it happen.

- **Change for Yourself:**

If you are setting a goal to change your life, don't do it because someone else wants you to do it; it will not work. No matter if it is your parents, girlfriend, boyfriend, coach, or anyone, you won't want it bad enough to make that change or that goal to stick. You have to want it. It is easy to stay on track if it is something you desire and want. If you do not want it, then your goal becomes an obligation.

- **Failing Does Not Mean Failure:**

Messing up does not mean you failed. It is part of the learning process. It is part of human nature. It is normal to mess up, but do not give up on your goal.

Now that you know a little about the goal-setting process, let's think about the vision you have for your life. Where do you want to be in five years? Ten years? Twenty years? What is the primary vision for the next year of your life? Knowing where you are going in life is the first step in getting there. Without vision, we just move aimlessly through life; we live without a purpose. Remember, to achieve long-term goals, you should write them out. Next, break them into short-term goals and write them again. Then write how you are going to achieve each short-term goal. Lastly, write rewards you can give yourself every time you achieve a goal. Now, I want you to write three goals you wish to accomplish in the next year, one goal for the next five years, and one goal for the next ten years in the space provided. Included is a worksheet that I created and use myself. Please make additional copies as needed. Decide which goals you'd like to develop further and use only one long-term goal per sheet. To help you get started, I've provided an example of one of my personal long-term goals.

3 Goals:

____

____

____

Five-Year Goal:

____

Ten-Year Goal:

____

Long-Term Goal: ______________________________

Short-Term Goals	Daily Steps	Rewards

EXAMPLE

Long-Term Goal: <u>2012 WRITE A BOOK and finish in 2013</u>

Short-Term Goals	Daily Steps	Rewards
Read books on how to write books. Work on it weekly. Sit and write anything every week. Set time to work on book every week. Talk to people who can help with the book: Rich, Fran, Pastor Get Microsoft Office for computers. Outline: Start writing. Just write; get as much stuff down as possible this year. Think about workbook to go along with book. Read other books for inspiration. Take notes.	Think about the book and the ideas for it every day. Write them down. Keep a folder of ideas. Write down scriptures that would fit in the book when I come across them. Be in the Spirit every time you write. Listen to inspirational music when you write.	After working on it for three weeks straight, take a week off to have fun. After finishing halfway, buy something you've been aching to buy for a long time. When the book is done, have a big dinner celebration with family and friends.

We've covered how important choices are in life and how to make the "right" choices, as well as how to create a vision and set goals. Now it leaves us with perhaps the single most important thing in life: finding your God-given purpose. Knowing your purpose will give us motivation. Motivation will bring desires, desires will stir drive, and drive will give us the energy to chase our purpose with full determination. Once you finally discover your purpose in life, you will have meaning and substance; you will feel a sense of fulfillment that you never thought was possible. To do this, you must pray, enter into worship, listen to worship music, and take some time to praise and worship God, all the while asking Him to help you discover your purpose. There are three worksheets to help you find your purpose, but you must put your heart and soul into each worksheet. I spent two hours on each, and then went back a week later and spent another two hours on the last worksheet. As I am fond of saying, this exercise will change your life. And it is true. ***If*** you open up to God and do each worksheet with all your heart and soul, you will find your God-given purpose in this world. These next three exercises on finding your purpose come from a teaching of Pastor John Carter from Abundant Life Christian Center in Syracuse, New York.

Purpose: Part One

List as many things as you can under each question. Just keep writing. Spend time on each of them.

1. Inspiration: What excites you?
2. Agitation: What bothers you?
3. Association: What relationships are you drawn to?
4. Endowment or Enablement: What are you naturally good at?
5. Accolade: What do others say I am good at?
6. Revelation: What has God spoken to you about doing?
7. Accident: We often "bump" into our purpose. List things in life that you bumped into.

Purpose: Part Two

Time Machine

End of your life. You are going to die in a few hours...

What have I experienced, achieved? Where have I been? Who have I spent time with?

How can you close your eyes for your last time in peace and go to heaven?

Imagine that you are now about to close your eyes for the very last time.

Write this over and over again: I wish I'd done, I wish I'd done, I wish I'd done, I wish I'd done.

Now list everything you wish you had done—spent time with, achieved, loved, or anything you need to write down—so you can close your eyes for the last time and be fulfilled and ready to die.

Purpose: Part Three

Finding Your Purpose

Reread the other two (2) purpose activities you've already completed.

1. **Get a piece of paper. Write, "My purpose in life is?" on top.**
2. **Now start writing without thinking. Just write, "My purpose is _____ and go ____________.**
3. **When you stop to think, write the sentence over again. "My purpose is to ______." There should be no stopping in this activity.**
4. **Don't stop writing until you feel a strong emotion inside over something you wrote. Break that down, and then narrow it down. Don't stop writing until you tear up or cry.**
5. **When that happens, you found your purpose. Put it into a sentence. "My purpose in life is to _________."**

The final step is to take your purpose in life that God has for you and surround it with vision that will lead you to your purpose. Write down your purpose and vision. Surround your purpose with short-term and long-term goals that will help you achieve it. Stop and think of every choice you make. Ask yourself, "Is this getting me closer or further away from my purpose?" If you want to be set free, you need vision, hope, and a purpose for your life. When you have those things, nothing can stop you.

Scriptures

Jeremiah 29:11 ESV

For I know the plans I have for you, declares the Lord, plans for welfare and not for evil, to give you a future and a hope.

Acts 26:16 ESV

But rise and stand upon your feet, for I have appeared to you for this purpose, to appoint you as a servant and witness to the things in which you have seen me and to those in which I will appear to you.

Romans 8:28 ESV

And we know that for those who love God all things work together for good, for those who are called according to his purpose.

Proverbs 16:9 ESV

The heart of man plans his way, but the Lord establishes his steps.

John 15:16

You did not choose me, but I chose you and appointed you that you should go and bear fruit and that your fruit should abide, so that whatever you ask the Father in my name, he may give it to you.

Matthew 28:19 ESV

Go therefore and make disciples of all nations, baptizing them in the name of the Father and of the Son and of the Holy Spirit.

Ephesians 1:11

In him we have obtained an inheritance, having been predestined according to the purpose of him who works all things according to the counsel of his will.

Chapter Ten
Amendment 10

Relationships (Maybe the Hardest Part)

Before we get started, I want you to list your five closest friends or family members—the people you spend most of your time with, those you talk to throughout the day or week.

1) ______________________
2) ______________________
3) ______________________
4) ______________________
5) ______________________

One of my favorite sayings is, "Show me your five closest friends, and I will show you your future." Another saying I like is, "You will never ever rise above your five closest friends." What do these sayings mean to you? What are they implying?

Trust me, this saying is completely correct. This is so true. I had different types of friends for different levels of my life. When I had friends who just wanted to sit around and chill, years that were full of chilling went by. I was not going to any place—I just existed. Then I got a group of friends who were criminals, ex-cons, and drug dealers. That was when my life was full of fights, drug dealing, and law breaking. However, after I surrounded myself with people who were climbing, or those who are almost done climbing, the same mountain of success I was climbing, I noticed how fast my life started to turn in that direction. Instead of going downhill, or—just as bad—staying in one place for years, I was finally moving up the mountain. And I can honestly say that I owe that to the people I surrounded myself with. I heard a saying once in my life, and to me this saying rings true. "In life, we have to decide what side of the mountain we want to die on." It means finding out what you want to live for and surround yourself with people going to the same place as you, or with those who already gotten there, then start climbing that mountain.

A very important key in getting set free is your relationships—cutting old friends (friends who deep down you already know are negative influences) out of your life and replacing them with new friends. Maybe you are saying something like, "You do not know what my friends are and what I have been through. You have no idea how important my friends are to me. There is no way I am turning my back on my friends. That is just not me. We've been through way too much." Believe me, I had all these feelings. I thought to myself, "There is no way in the world I will ever cut my old friends out of my life." However, God had other plans for me. If you do not cut them out of your life, God will. Just so you know, cutting them out does not mean you will stop caring for them or loving them.

This chapter will talk about relationships and why you should get negative people out of your life. I will use personal experiences as examples and will tell you about my "old" friends and how God cut them out of my life. Then I will talk about the importance of positive relationships and "community" in God's eyes. I will also give examples of how my life changed drastically as soon as I added new relationships in my life, people I could look up to.

Aside from family, there was nothing more important to me than friends. If you met my "crew," you met me. We all behaved the same for the most part. Growing up, I moved a lot, so friends would come and go. But when I was in seventh grade, my family somehow began to settle in one area (though I moved a few more times after I graduated in high school). That was when I became part of a set of friends that I kept until my mid-thirties. This group would be considered my new family. As a matter of fact, when my grandma died, they sat with me for the entire day. When my mom died, they stayed with me for the entire week. One in particular moved in with me because he was afraid I would try to end my life. These weren't just my friends. These people were my blood. If one fought, we all fought. If one hurt, we all hurt. If one laughed, we all laughed. If one cried, we all cried. You get the point? It's amazing to note that as close as we were, we all picked on each other and were very negative towards one another. If you have friends like these, let me just say right now that no matter how much you love them, you may have to cut them out of your life like a cancer. Given enough time, their negativity and behaviors will spread throughout your body, eating away at your soul, mind, and heart, causing a death that can be far worse than physical death.

The Bible says in Proverbs 12:26, "The righteous should *choose* his friends carefully, for the way of the wicked leads them ASTRAY." This scripture reeks of truth. I encourage all of you to memorize this scripture, meditate on it, and confess it daily.

This is an example of how you gravitate to the level your friends are at. In my mid-twenties, I had a different set of friends whom most of my "family friends" didn't even know about. These friends were professional criminals. Most have been in and out of prison, and the ones who haven't been just haven't gotten caught. Once I was having a problem with a person who was threatening to take me to court. I told this new group of friends about this situation, and they told me to come back to their place later that night. I did. I was told to sit down. I heard, "So you have a problem?" I explained my problem. I then heard, "This one is free. What do you want to happen? Do you want this person dead? Missing? Or just warned?" No smiles, no laughs, just silence. I loved this power, this way of life. I remember thinking to myself that I have a group of friends who can finally take me to a place in life that I have always dreamed of.

Another story of my new friends happened while I was outside a club. I see this man who was talking a lot of stuff about me a few weeks ago; he wanted to fight me. This man was very large and probably used steroids (it was a fact he uses steroids). So I said to my friend, "I will be right back. I am going to talk to this dude and see if there is still a problem (I did this because I didn't want to get sucker-punched at the club by this guy)." I started to walk across the street alone towards this guy, and I noticed my boy walking behind me. He's not saying a word; he just stood behind me. The man I was going to question knew who and what type of connections this man who stood behind me had. The respect I got from the very large man was the type of respect you offer to presidents and royalty. Hanging out with this type of people corrupted my thoughts. I thought nobody could ever touch me, so I could do whatever I wanted. I feared nothing and said whatever I wanted to say to whoever I wanted to say it. I became the five people I hung out most with. I started to gamble all the time; poker felt like my calling in life. I would play poker five times a week, staying up all night. I bet on football, basketball, you name it. I would win playing poker then lose betting on football. I would go to the casino and spend ten hours playing poker. I spent months learning how to read people and how to cheat at shuffling. Then I would practice those "tricks" on my friends so I could perfect it in real games. I truly loved gambling. I would take advantage of anyone at any time for their money. My fantasy became my reality because of my peers. All my friends were criminals and gamblers, and this is what I became. This opened the doors that would lead me to a road that only Jesus can bring someone back from.

One door that opened for me was drug dealing. I sometimes wonder if drug dealing was in our family bloodline, because it came so easy for me, so natural. I mean, just like families that are generations of businessmen, policemen, Army men, politicians, lawyers, teachers, etc. It was the hardest struggle in my life to get away from, and out of all sins, it is the hardest not to turn back to. As I wrote this book, God revealed why drug dealing was so attractive to me. It was simple. People who do drugs need a drug dealer. So I felt needed, wanted. I felt that people have to have me around. Now let's break that down another level. I felt loved in a way. So what does that mean? For me, drug dealing gave me a false sense of love. Love brings freedom, but a false sense of love brings captivity, lack of hope, and depression.

I knew that the man who lived next door to me was an alcoholic, but he could not buy beer with his food stamps. So he approached me one day and said, "If you buy me a case of beer, I will give you this bottle of pills." I read the pill bottle: OxyContin, 30 milligrams. I could not believe my eyes knowing that I could sell them for a dollar a milligram and that the market on oxys at this time was giant. I turned a fifteen-dollar beer investment into a 1,500-dollar profit. After a year of this, I soon started to sell oxys, hydrocodone, muscle relaxers, valium, morphine, Xanax, and even Viagra on a regular basis. Every month I would get these drugs.. The connection I made with the guy who lived next door caused me to hang out with him more and the more. Then I hung out with more people like him who had more drugs and looking to trade for oxys or beer. I'll say again, show me your five closest friends, and I will show you your future. It was like there were two sides of me for my two different groups of friends. I would never let the two groups mix.

After a few years of selling these drugs, of course, I had to try some. I won't go into details because I've already shared my life of drug abuse previously. I cannot say this enough: if you want to be set free in this life, you must take a look at your relationships and—in most cases—end them. I know it sounds harsh, but if they are not God-fearing people walking with Jesus, then you should not be at their level; they will just drag you down to their level. To explain this, I thought about an exercise that I do with my youth group at church. (This will help paint a picture for you.) Have one youth stand on a tiny child chair, and then ask a bigger, stronger youth to stand next to him or her on the floor. Tell the youth on the floor to pull down the smaller youth standing on the chair until he or she is off the chair. After that, ask the smaller youth on the chair to pull the bigger, stronger youth on the floor up to "his or her level" onto the chair. While it takes less effort for the bigger, stronger youth to drag down the smaller youth on the tiny chair, it needs a lot of power on the part of the smaller youth to pull up the bigger, stronger youth on the chair. This shows that it is a lot easier to be brought back down when you are around friends who bring you down than it is to stay up where Jesus wants you.

The guys I grew up with—whom I talked about in the beginning of the chapter—were my best friends in the world. In fact, I did not call them "friends"; I called them "family." As a matter of fact, if we were out, I would introduce them to people as my cousins. I even called their parents "Mom" and "Dad." The entire group became best of friends, so it made it easier to always hang out. There were four of us in this group. We did everything together. After high school, one of my best friends and I drove down to California together twice. The rest of us took vacations (called "mancations") when we were in our late twenties. Now I am telling this story to illustrate how separating yourself from old relationships can be the hardest step in your life. This was a very worldly but good group of guys. They all knew my mom, and my mom adored them all. One of them helped rebuild her kitchen and living room when I was in college. When my mom passed away, this was my family. I would spend Christmas, Thanksgiving, and most holidays at one of their houses. I loved this group of friends and would have died for anyone of them.

I am now in my thirties—free from the things of my past, going to church, serving, preaching, or conducting Bible studies. I am engulfed in the word of God. When I decided to focus on my spiritual works, I began spending less and less time with my old group of friends. It's not by choice, just the way life works, although we would still spend every Friday night or Saturday night together then. Soon I started to only make once-a-month hang outs, then once-every-three-months type of thing. They were still my best friends; I still love them to death. But inside I started hearing the Spirit of God saying, "You need to separate yourself from them; they are not going where you are going." (Surround yourself with the five people you want to be like.) I ignored the voice inside but noticed that I was spending less and less time with them. On the other hand, I was spending more and more time with a different group of people whom I will talk about in the next chapter. Our differences started to become more prevalent than our common interests. They drink; I don't. They go to bars and pick up women; I don't. They swear, but I don't swear anymore. So when we did hang out, it was different than it used to be.

Then one day, after about a year has passed since I've seen my group of "family," we decided to all get together and play a game of poker like we use to. Now I am fully into Jesus at this point. I said to myself that even though I didn't gamble anymore, I would go and play a game just for fun because I miss these guys so much. So I was actually excited about this get-together. I truly was going just for the fellowship of my friends. Regarding the poker game part, I thought to myself that as long as I just play for fun, it's "OK."

So I did show up. One of my best friends couldn't attend, and there were two other men whom I'd seen but didn't really "know." Everyone was already drinking, so the friendly insults to each other were flowing. I ignored the indirect jabs about my being a Christian—implications of being "better than," different. We were having fun, right? The night went on. We decided it was time to play poker. This was when things took a turn for the worse. One of my friends started to pretend he's a televangelist and began to fake preach. I tried to ignore him. Another one started to denigrate Jesus and questioned why I was "gambling" and just won't let up. I lost my temper and my ability to be an effective witness for these individuals. I threatened to punch the kid who was talking, then I threatened to punch another one. Every other word I spoke was a swear word, and I was yelling out of my mouth. Being the toughest kid in the neighborhood (mentality), I challenged them all to take me on. My best friend said, "See, Colby, you always have to start fights. You never will change." For the first time in my life, my friend told me to leave his house and I was not welcome there anymore. That is the last time I talked to him and had seen any of them. I realized that God had already told me to separate myself from them, and I should have listened. I learned it the hard way, and to this day, it still is one of the hardest things I ever had to do. I still love them all and care for them, but I am just on a different path in life now.

Old friends, anybody with whom you used to do negative things or who instilled negative thoughts and disturbed your peace—you need to get them out of your life. But cutting people out of your life does not mean you have to stop loving them or praying for them. It just may mean you cannot surround yourself with them.

As you walk with God, you will notice changes starting in you. This change is wonderful. God starts to work on you, changing your heart, mind, actions, and way of speech. It is true that there will come a time when four-letter words just do not taste as good when they come out of your mouth. This change will cause some friends to just disappear, fade away, or slowly but surely walk out of your life. One day you will wake up and say, "Wow, whatever happened to so and so?" Some friends do it without being seen. They will wait until you are not paying attention, and then sneak out the back door. Others do it without reason but without hiding either. You will call them, but they will not answer. You will text them, but they will not reply. You will send them a Facebook message, but they will not answer. After a few months of this kind of action, take the hint. None of them will tell you to your face that they do not like what you stand for, but they will say it with their actions. You will still love them, but when you look around, they are nowhere to be found. They think you've changed. They will say things like, "You think you are better than me? You keep judging me," when, in fact, you never spoke to them about God or even once corrected their behaviors. They just feel that condemnation because you are walking right and people see that and are intimidated by the way you walk. God warned us of this happening, so it should not come to us as a shock. That being said, it still hurts. John 15:18 says, "If the world hates you, know it hated me first." Psalm 27:10 says, "For my father and mother have forsaken me, but the Lord will take me in." In John 1:11 it is written: "He came to his own, and his own people did not receive him." The Bible is clear. It tells us that if we do not pick up our own cross and follow Him, then we are not worthy of Him. When you pick up your cross, you will see friends part ways from you like the Red Sea.

On the other hand, we need people in our lives. God created us to be communal creatures, to have relationships. So in the next chapter, I will talk about what kind of relationships we are supposed to have. Even Jesus, the Son of God, did not do it alone; he had relationships, the Apostles.

Scriptures

Proverbs 12:26

The righteous should choose his friends carefully, for the way of the wicked leads them astray.

Note: We are righteous (born again). We need to choose who we spend our time with or take counsel from, because if you are not righteous, then you are of the world. And worldly people can/will lead you away from God.

2 Corinthians 6:14

Do not be unequally yoked together with unbelievers. For what fellowship has righteousness with lawlessness? And what communion has light with dark?

Proverbs 13:20

He who walks with wise men will be wise but the companion of fools will be destroyed.

Chapter Eleven
AMENDMENT 11

Mentors, Peers, Mentees

Your ***circle of influence*** needs to be in full motion to produce power and change in your life.

Getting free is going to take sacrifices. You need to ask yourself, "How badly do I want to be free? How badly do I want to change? How sick am I of this life? Will I do whatever it takes to become a new person free from spiritual death and hopelessness?" I once heard a saying that I love: "In order for us to truly change, we need to change *the way* we change." This is so true because many of us have changed throughout our lives, but we keep on going back to our old ways. We never really "changed." So if we change the way we change, then we can have everlasting "change." There is only one way to begin to change *the way* you change, and that is looking towards Jesus. When you slip, cry out to Jesus and thank Him for his Mercy and Grace. You will not be able to do any of these amendments to its fullest on your own. You need to look up to Jesus for each step and ask Him to show you how to fulfill it. Ask Him for His help and strength. I hope that at this point in the book, you are truly ready to change *the way* you change and truly commit to these amendments. I stressed this point now on this amendment because you truly need the help of the Holy Spirit for this step.

Amendment 11 is about finding new friends. We talked about cutting away all our old friends in chapter ten. Now this amendment will instruct you on how to replace those people with God-fearing and wise people—people you can look up to, learn from, and be mentored by. Get a group of friends with the same goals and visions that you have, so you can talk about those goals and visions and how to reach them. You need supportive relationships. This was explained to me by one of my best friends and mentors this way: you need to be like a waterwheel. This is a machine for converting the energy of free-flowing or falling water into useful forms of power. Now, picture a giant waterwheel. If you do not know what one is, picture a big wooden or metal wheel with a number of blades or buckets arranged on the outside. As water fills each bucket, the wheel starts to turn around and around. Water is coming in and going out, and sustaining. Similarly, if we want to be useful or full of power, we need to be like the waterwheel. We need to have three groups of positive friends. One group that will pour into us (fill our buckets) are our mentors. We call on them for wisdom or knowledge. We see how they handled events in life. We look up to them on how to become better men or women of God. Then we need a group that maintains us (the transition before the bucket empties). This group is for us to talk to, share common goals and visions with, and contemplate ideas with on how to get to those goals and visions. This group is used to pick each other up and encourage each other. The last group is a group of people we pour into (when the buckets empty themselves out on their way down the circle into the stream). This group looks up to you. They use you as mentors. This way, we are constantly growing. And while we are growing, we are sowing into others as well. It is a circle. I call this the *circle of influence*. Below, I have given you some room to describe your circle of influence. If you already have some people in your life who mentor you or you mentor, write them on the space provided. If not, I want you to pray and ask the Holy Spirit to reveal at least two people (in each stage of the circle) to you. You need your circle of influence to be in full motion to produce power and change in your life.

My Personal Circle of Influence

Mentors Filling You Up:

____

____

____

____

Peers Maintaining You:

____

____

____

____

Mentees You Are Filling Up:

____

____

____

____

Mentors are those people whom you allow to speak into your life, who have been through life and through wars and know how to battle. They are spiritual fathers and mothers. We need to cherish the mentors and honor them. They are people who want to build you up, not tear you down. When we look at the word of God, we have seen numerous times that a man of God was linked with another to learn from them and to be a partner in what they are doing. Examples are: Elijah and Elisha, David and Jonathan, Naomi and Ruth. Jesus called men, one by one, and made them disciples (mentored them), so they could go out and do the same. Mentoring is really another term for discipleship. If you are sinning, they are not afraid to call you out in a loving way and tell you that you are messing up. That is how much a mentor cares about you. I will use three different stories that happened to me and the three different mentors in my life.

Mentor #1 Story: This particular mentor was one of my best friends. He was speaking to me about life, things he has heard or seen, and things I have told him about this girl I was seeing. I'd just rededicated my life to Christ, and it was in that first year of walking with Him when this issue came up. The girl I was seeing was married (though she told me, she was separated and getting a divorce), and our relationship did not line up with the word of God at all. This girl brought me so much pain and torment; I could not understand how God could allow me to be in a relationship like that. My mentor told me that this girl was going to be the death of me. He was not joking. These are strong words for someone to say, and he believed them and said them with conviction and power. He said he sensed it from the Lord. Of course, like a good mentee, I did not listen. I *heard* him but I didn't listen, because I continued to see her. Even so, I continued to pray for wisdom from God on what to do. Remember the chapter on choices? We want what we want, and I wanted her. God bless my mess. We all do it.

(Side note: Just so you all know, God can yell the answer at you and put it in front of your face, or have thirty different people come to you and tell you the answer. But if you truly do not want to hear it, you won't. Looking back, I see so many signs that I should have cut off all communications with her. But at that time, I didn't want to, and I suffered the hurt from it. Sometimes we just have to step out in faith and listen to the advice of those who have authority over us. A good leader surrounds himself with people who are smarter

than he is. After that, a good leader listens to the advice of those people even if he disagrees. Thinking back, I should have listened to my mentor and just walked away; it would have saved me a year of pain and misery.)

Anyway, I ignored his advice and kept seeing this girl. Now, I am trying to represent being a good Christian. When her "husband" found out, he hated me, and we had a verbal disagreement. And we all know that I don't do too well with words. My actions give Christianity a bad name. I am supposed to be representing God here on earth. Once again my opportunity to be a witness was lost. Wanting to fight and being drunk all slowly returned to my life. This woman was filling me with so much anger by not talking to me, having other men over, and saying she loved me then taking it back. It was destroying me. That time she told me about a situation I cannot go into in this book out of respect and privacy was one of the final straws. Basically, I felt the need to protect her, and the old me started to really come back. I started to make phone calls to people who can assist me in taking care of problems.

Every Bible verse, every still, small voice and blaring alarm that the Holy Spirit was sending were lost. My flesh was in control. This event was bigger than I am. The old "me"—the old image that hadn't been fully restructured—was in control. I needed help. I needed someone stronger in the Lord. The Bible says that in every temptation, the Lord will offer a means of escape. My spirit was still just long enough to find my lifeline. Something inside me said, "Calm down. Call your mentor and talk to him." We met for coffee, and I told him about what happened and what I was going to do. Now he knew I was serious because he was one of my best friends. He knew both the born-again Colby and the drug-dealing/rapper/fighting Colby. He told me I was wrong and that God would handle it. I told him I do not have time for God to handle this, and I don't want to dispel any chance that He won't handle this. He continued to talk to me that day about what a bad idea it was. He looked at me and didn't judge but wasn't shocked; he just spoke wisdom into my life. He made me realize how I was not behaving like Jesus would, and how the story may not be completely true. He reminded me of how he said she would be the death of me, and if I did do that thing, I would be dead. By representing Jesus in the flesh, that mentor saved my life that day. He was there when I needed him. *(Side note: This incident took place before my written confession exercise that I talked about in chapter three. That exercise set me completely free from the old me, and I believe it will do the same to you.)*

Sometimes mentors will speak into your life about things you may or may not agree on. But you put this mentor into your life; therefore you need to listen with respect and truly think over their suggestions or advice. Many million-dollar corporations have a board of directors that can look from the outside in and give people real advice. Many times they may not agree with the board's advice, but they have to remember that it's not real advice if they only tell what people want to hear or want to do. Mentors were put in place for a reason, and I suggest you use them if you want to grow yourself into the billion-dollar corporation God wants you to be.

Mentor #2 Story: This story took place when I was far along in my walk with God. I was ministering at different places throughout the week, teaching a class for the church that I attended in, and serving as the armor bearer of the head pastor of the church. On the day of this event, I was at home at about 7:00 a.m. I got a phone call from a former coworker. First, let me explain that this coworker was a Christian woman, a single mom, who moved in from out of town and had no family or friends in this city. She was my friend; she would help me with money when I was broke or let me borrow her car if mine was broken. She was and still is a good Christian woman. At this time, she was seeing a man who was a self-admitted former drug dealer recently released (about eighteen months) from prison. He was working when she met him and trying to change his life. What she didn't know was that he was also an avid drug user and would constantly return to jail. She was too trusting. And just like my story with Mentor #1, she was hearing the warnings of others but wasn't ready to listen. Now, on this particular day, this man had borrowed her car. But three days later, there was no car, no boyfriend—nothing. He was not answering his phone. He was not at home or at any other friend's house. Nothing. He was just missing, along with my friend's car. So she asked me for help to drive her around, looking for her car early that morning. I told her I would only help if she was willing to call the cops on him and tell them that her car was stolen. She told me she had, but they couldn't do anything about the car. They said they looked for it and could not find it or him. So I got up at 7:00 a.m. and went to pick her up. We then started to look for her car. About an hour of looking and finding nothing, I said, "OK, you happy? I am going to drop you off now." As soon as I said that, we saw two men come out of some apartment and got into her car. I did a U-turn and started to follow them. They noticed and started to run red lights and make illegal turns. But I continued to follow. I told my coworker, "Call the police." She got through and was telling them what street we saw them on, but at this point I'd lost them. So I made another turn and saw them at a red light. We jumped out and opened the door and "took" the car back. The man went out, and she jumped in and took off. I jumped in my car and took off, too. So, basically, we carjacked a carjacker. I got home and made a Facebook post summarizing the details of our crazy morning.

I received a telephone call that evening from Mentor #2 inviting me over for a cup of coffee. I accepted. When I arrived, we went up to his pool house and sat and began to talk about life. He then said, "I need to address something with you, Colby." He reminded me that I was a leader in the church and people look up to me. So putting the message I did on Facebook was not a smart idea. I could have been killed. Then he said, "It gives people a bad image of you and makes younger kids think that what you did was cool, and they may want to try something like that and then get hurt. He continued to say that I was acting too much like my old self and that was a dangerous ground to be walking on. I took in what he said. At this point, you have two choices: respond out of your flesh and old nature, or respond in the way God would want you to and say, "Thank you for the advice. I guess you're right. I didn't look at it that way, so thank you for showing me a different way to look at the situation." Like I said, before you—or should I say God—chose the mentors in your life, you allowed them the right to speak into your life.

Relationships are complex things, and although your mentor is typically more mature and a bit more grounded in their Christian walk, the Bible promises that we will all suffer trials and tribulations. There will come a time when they will hit a wall or go through a trail. You may be the only person they have to help them stand, and you may be the only person who cares enough to build them back up so they can fight again. When this happens, you better be prepared and ready to go to war with them. A friend loves at all times, and a brother is born for adversity (Proverbs 17:17). Be aware, because when it does happen, it will not only build character in your life, but it will bring you to new levels in your walk with God. Here's my example.

Mentor #3 Story: If it wasn't for this particular mentor, I would not have made it through many of my trials in life. I am convinced that God put him in my life, so I did not give up on him. For many times I would have returned back to drug dealing or just gave up, but this mentor did not allow that to even be an option. I was living in a situation where a lot of bad things were taking place inside the house, not to mention that the house was also undergoing foreclosure. It got to the point where I had chosen sleeping in my car over going home. Mentor #3 offered me an apartment that he owned for next to nothing. It came at the perfect time for the perfect price. As a matter of fact, he asked me how much I wanted to spend. I told him, and then he took off an extra hundred dollars.

It still amazes me when looking back on how much God took care of me. There was a time when I got laid off from my job and what did this mentor do? He told me not to pay rent anymore until I find a new job. Then after I found a new one, he told me, "Now catch up on your bills." Then I got laid off again and got a part-time job in the ministry preaching to teens, and he told me not to pay rent till I get a full-time job. God worked through this man in ways that the world would not understand. To top it off, for over a year, this man would give me money to pay for bills or to buy food whenever I saw him. One day this mentor came up to me and said that God spoke to him and told him to pay off all my credit card debt. God is truly amazing when you let him work through other people and other people let him work through them.

Mentor #3 hit a wall one year, and when I say hit a wall, just imagine a scenario where he found himself in the middle of a shark-infested ocean during a storm with no boat. I told him, "I will fight with you side by side. Because God is bigger than this world, He is bigger than our circumstances; He can make the impossible possible." So as a good friend of this man, we decided on our war strategy, which involved trusting in God, but we wanted to put some action to this trust. So to help with his stress, we decided to wake up every day at 4:30 a.m., meet at the gym, and then go prayer walk (walking while praying). We chose to use Joshua 6:1–27 as our guiding principle; most of you will have heard the story about the wall of Jericho. I don't know about you, but the idea of getting up every day at 4:30 to lift weights and then pray was not my idea of fun. But I was committed to fight this war with my friend. He had been a mentor for years, and it was the least I could do. So for months, we did this every day. We walked in the summer and in the winter, when it was hot and when it was freezing. We marched and prayed for supernatural favor, for God's will to be done. We stood side by side. I fought with my brother, I laughed with him, cried with him, and spoke God's word with him. Like I said earlier, a good friend—a friend who is for you—is ready to fight for you at any time in any place without asking a question. A true friend does not need a reason; they just suit up and go to war with you. God showed himself real to this mentor of mine during this period in ways that only God can.

Maintain Group (Peers): The second group of people in our lives that we need is a group that helps us to maintain. (Remember our waterwheel analogy? This is the transition before the bucket empties) This group is for us to talk to, share common goals with, and discuss ideas on how to get to our vision. These people support and encourage one another. This group helps you sustain your current level, and it grows with you. The perfect cycle has the maintainers following the mentors, then the mentees help the maintainers from slipping backwards. Your maintenance friends/family should be the primary source of support you should meet often, work together with, live together with, and pray together with, holding each other up. Sometimes, over the years, your mentors can become a part of your maintenance group, and there is nothing wrong with that.

Maintain Story One: This is a perfect example of what you should be doing with this group. One of my maintainers and I decided to host a monthly group (prayer) breakfast. We would get a group of guys together once a month to eat, fellowship, and then pray for not only each other, but also our community, our church, and the world. This also gave us all an opportunity to open up and talk about what we are struggling with and keep each other accountable while praying for each other. A good maintainer relationship involves motivating each other, and every member should be at the same level spiritually because you want to grow together to the next level.

I have so many examples of using my maintainer, because if you are using this the way it is supposed to be, you will be in contact throughout the week. So you can cut off temptation before it births into sin. One of the hardest desires for me to overcome through my years of growing as a Christian and through my years of preaching and ministering was the desire to sell drugs again. I would go through times in life when I was unemployed, bills were due, and my phone would not stop ringing because bill collectors nag me. This period in my life happened more than once; it happened a lot. In my head, I would think, "Don't worry. Just go make some money the way you used to." When I say this was a big temptation for me, I mean it would come into my head and take months to fight away. If I ponder on it for a few days, then it could take even longer. I would even find myself every now and again driving around my old neighborhood just to see who I could see.

If it was not for my maintainer group, I do not know if I could have made it through. This group is so important because you can talk about each other's struggles and agree to pray for each other. Also, as soon as you bring your temptation into the light, you take all power away from it—no longer does it have power over you.

The final group is called mentees. This is the group in which you pour yourself into. I grew up without having a mentor; therefore I was never a mentee because my dad left when I was twelve years old. I never had a positive male to look up to. I never had anyone to teach me how to shave or how to shake hands. My mom had to talk to me about sex. I had no man to teach me how to be a man or even how to tie a tie. I spent my teen years trying to be the man my dad never taught me to be. In school, I misbehaved because I had no dad at home to tell me not to or to believe in me. I remember in eleventh grade, a teacher took me to the side and said, "Colby, you are one of the smartest students I ever met in my life. These people you are entertaining in class will not be there for you in a few years. If you applied yourself, you could be a straight A student." That teacher changed my life just from that little talk. For the first time, I had a male figure speak positivity into my life and believe in me. He was the reason I went to college. A few seconds out of this guy's day changed my entire life. He was my first mentor. It was also the first time I felt how good it was to be a mentee. I truly believe we are doing our best in this life when we are mentoring someone else. We are going to reproduce ourselves into other people who will one day go out and do the same to other people. When I started youth pastoring, a wise man once told me that I needed to find one or two kids in my youth group who would stand out to me. "Take those two and pour yourself into them, mentor them, give them all you have and watch them go out and change that entire youth group." People feed off what other people feed them. We learn from others. That is why we go to school. This is why the Bible has disciples. This is how we pass on things to other generations.

I also find it a great way to stay motivated to do the right thing. I, for one, am less likely to want to let someone else down. I could care less about letting myself down, but put a kid in my life to be mentored and the last thing I want to do is fall short of that young person's expectation. Granted we will fall short, that is life, but I am talking about extra motivation to persevere. Suppose I am a Christian and I am not mentoring anyone, I may find it "OK" to go to the bar and have a few drinks. But if I am mentoring a kid, I do not want him to ever find out that I'm going to a bar, so I would be more likely to stay away from those situations. **While mentors tell mentees how to walk that straight line, mentees keep the mentors walking a straight line.**

How to mentor a mentee? Simply let them see you "walk it out." Live your life as an open example. Offer them alternatives without preaching and or lecturing them. I remember one young man I mentored. He was a great kid, very well-known, and thought he had all the answers in the world. He loved to challenge you (my type of kid). Now this kid was going to church but didn't really believe in God. He loved to drink and smoke weed. He loved to go to parties and hit on women. His parents asked me if I could get coffee with him and talk to him. So I did, and we hit it off right away. When he told me all that he was into and how he didn't believe in

God, I did not panic, did not judge, or ask, "What do you mean? You grew up in the church." Instead, I met him where he was and related to his experiences and where that road could lead—things like that. We met every week for about three years. I started to challenge him, telling him that instead of smoking every day, he should try to smoke three times a week. (This is a controversial therapeutic principle called "harm reduction.") He would do it; eventually, he stopped smoking and drinking. Then he got saved (asked Jesus into his heart). Since that day, he has been growing, changing—basically becoming his own man. It is a blessing to see.

Why is this amendment so important? Because even deeper than mentoring is the constant relationship God created us to be in. Think about it. God is the ultimate example of relationship. He has given us His Spirit to guide us and His Son to plea for us. HE is our Father. That is how important relationships are. We need that connection to move on, to get where we want to go. God builds partnerships, and so does Satan—he even knows how important they are. Until Jesus returns, this world is Satan's playground. Therefore, we as Christians need to have a community of support to defeat him and his attacks. To get things done, you need partnerships. The Bible says that a three-fold cord is not easily broken. (Ecclesiastes 4:12) When people get together, there is nothing we cannot do or achieve. To get to the next level in our life, we don't need money or degrees; we need other relationships. (I am not down playing money and degrees. I am just trying to make a point.) That is how you get to the next level. People around you are connected to your destiny. Jesus the Son of God did not do it alone; he had relationships, the Apostles. Jesus got to the next level of his ministry through another person: John the Baptist baptized him. I promise you that doors will open for you through your relationships. I cannot tell you how many jobs I obtained because of relationships. Think about it. Nobody wanted Paul to be allowed into the inner circle of the disciples. Nobody trusted him because he was a murderer of Christians. But one person, one relationship, brought Paul in—and that was Barnabas. Barnabas vouched for him, brought him to the church leaders, and said that he was a changed man. Who knows? If it were not for Barnabas, half of the New Testament would not have been written.

In 1 Peter chapter 2:5 it says, "You are Living stones that God is building into his spiritual temple." God compares us to a stone, a building material. We are living stones. A stone isolated has very little value. If you go out to the parking lot and see a bunch of stones lying on the ground, there is not much value or purpose for them. But if you look at a building worth millions of dollars, you can see that it came together because of a lot of little stones. God said we are all living stones. It means that He intends to build something with us, and the way to build it is with other people.

Scriptures

Proverbs 11:14

Where there is no counsel, the people fall; but in the multitude of counselors there is safety.

Proverbs 19:20

Listen to counsel and receive instruction, that you may be wise in your latter days.

Proverbs 13:20

He who walks with wise men will be wise, but the companion of fools will be destroyed.

Proverbs 24:5

A wise man is strong, yes, a man of knowledge increases strength; for by wise counsel you will wage your own war, and in a multitude of counselors there is safety.

Proverbs 27:17

As iron sharpens iron, so a man sharpens the countenance of his friend.

Psalm 145:3-4

Great is the Lord, and greatly to be praised; and His greatness is unsearchable. One generation shall praise Your works to another, And shall declare Your mighty acts.

Chapter Twelve
Amendment 12

Volunteering vs. Serving

This concept is going to seem so easy that it's common sense and self-explanatory. However, the majority of people don't do it. Research shows that on average, only about 20 percent of a church body volunteer at their local church. That means 80 percent just go to church, while a very small portion actually takes time out of their schedule to give back to the church and volunteer. Remember, in the last chapter, I talked about relationships; I talked about pouring into people, having people pour into you, and having people that maintain with you. Volunteering in your local church opens this door. To me this is the best opportunity to grow in your walk with Jesus because you are walking with other people to help other people.

Volunteering opened the door for me to change; it made me feel connected and a part of the church, not just a guest who comes in on Sunday and leaves. It made me feel important, needed, and loved, and it gave me the opportunity to make friends. I am not going to say volunteering *can* change your life; I am going to say volunteering ***will*** change your life, no question about it.

Volunteering will get you to connect, and connecting will build relationships. Relationships in turn will help bring you closer to Jesus. This amendment will set you free because volunteering will bring you new friends who will love on you, and love is what will set you free from any bondage that you are facing.

Now let me clear something up. I do not call myself a volunteer; I am a servant of God. This is how you have to look at serving God in your local church. "Servant" is mentioned in the Bible over 1,000 times; it is a very big deal. When Paul introduced himself in Romans 1:1, he says: "Paul, a servant of Christ Jesus." He is a servant, not a volunteer. Let me ask you: are you a servant or a volunteer? A volunteer picks whether to serve or not; a servant serves no matter what. A volunteer serves when convenient; a servant serves out of commitment to God.

Jesus did not recruit volunteers; he recruited servants. Everyone reading this book is a servant of God. I know it's time-consuming, difficult, and stressful, but it is who we are called to be. How do people see you?—as a servant trying to equip other people to grow and be faithful followers, or do they see you as someone who helps out every once in a while?

When you start to serve other people, you will be set free. Perhaps for the first time in years or your entire life, you will feel like you have a purpose. And that purpose will drive you and motivate you. It will bring joy and peace into your life. If you start serving others, you will notice that you will start to deny yourself—you will become less self-centered. The Lord gives us a similar blueprint in Matthew 16:24–25: [24]Then Jesus said to His disciples, "If anyone wishes to come after Me, he must deny himself, and take up his cross and follow Me. [25]"For whoever wishes to save his life will lose it; but whoever loses his life for My sake will find it." Every New Year, we make a list of resolutions that we end up breaking three days later. Why? Because we are trying to do it in our own strength—through sheer willpower. This never works. The only way to deny yourself is to fill yourself up with something else. Look at the word of God. Jesus says, "If anyone wishes to come after me, he must deny himself, and take up his cross and follow me." If we really want to deny ourselves, we need to let go of all our own desires, thoughts, sins, and behaviors and fill up with Jesus. If we are thinking about Jesus all the time and consume ourselves with him, our failures and shortcomings won't have such a hold over us, because it is all about Jesus. When you put other people's desires ahead of you, then you are truly serving Jesus. Serving Jesus will give you a new purpose, a new passion, and a new desire, and it will all be geared around him. Your life will be so intertwined with Jesus that you will talk about him to everyone. You will want to share His word and love with other people. You will also want to serve Him in your local church to get to know Him more and to be closer to Him and His people.

Let's look at a biblical example from Acts 4:32–35. This passage first discusses a group of 3,000 people. But by the fourth chapter , it states that there were over 6,000 people living together with the same heart and soul. They had all sold their land, houses, animals, and properties for the benefit of the entire community. Nothing they possessed was their own. These people all put the needs of others in front of their own. They lived life consumed with Jesus; they followed Jesus so that they didn't have any thoughts of their own needs. They just thought about how they can serve others.

If you start living this way, serving in your local church or in your community, your life will change. You will become fulfilled and joyful, with a sense of purpose. You will surrender to the Savior. Choose to be a servant rather than a volunteer, and I promise that you will find a new, more enjoyable life.

Scriptures:

Acts 4:32–35

32 Now the full number of those who believed were of one heart
and soul, and no one said that any of the things that belonged
to him was his own, but they had everything in common. 33 And
with great power the Apostles were giving their testimony to
the resurrection of the Lord Jesus, and great grace was upon
them all. 34 There was not a needy person among them, for as
many as were owners of lands or houses sold them and brought
the proceeds of what was sold 35 and laid it at the Apostles' feet,
and it was distributed to each as any had need.

Matthew 16:24–25

24 Then said Jesus unto his disciples, If any man will come after
me, let him deny himself, and take up his cross, and follow me.
25 For whosoever will save his life shall lose it: and whosoever
will lose his life for my sake shall find it.

Galatians 5:13

It is absolutely clear that God has called you to a free life. Just make sure that you don't use this freedom as an excuse to do whatever you want to do and destroy your freedom. Rather, use your freedom to serve one another in love; that's how freedom grows.

John 12:26

If any of you wants to serve me, then follow me. Then you'll be where I am, ready to serve at a moment's notice. The Father will honor and reward anyone who serves me.

Chapter Thirteen
Amendment 13

Stop Wasting Time

"By 2015, it is estimated that Americans will consume both traditional and digital media for over 1.7 trillion hours, an average of approximately 15 and a half hours per person per day. The amount of media delivered will exceed 8.75 zettabytes annually, or 74 gigabytes—9 DVDs worth—of data sent to the average consumer on an average day. A zettabyte is 10 raised to the 21st power bytes, a million gigabytes. These estimates are from an analysis of more than 30 different sources of media data, ranging from traditional media (TV, Radio, Voice telephone) to new digital sources (tablet computers, mobile gaming devices, smartphones, mobile video). Media consumed while at work is not included." ("How Much Media? 2013: Report on American Consumers," *James E. Short*).

Before we go further, I want to challenge you with an activity. I want you to document, just for a week, the amount of TV you watch and non-work-related computer time you use (PCs, iPads, cell phones) for video games, texting, Internet surfing, etc. Use the space below to document your media use. This is a self-reflective activity that I strongly suggest you do. Some of you will be amazed. I also recommend that you don't deliberately try to watch less or change anything. Just document what you normally do on a day-to-day basis. Carry this book with you, and every time you turn on the TV or you are at work and decide to visit Facebook for a little while, record it. I promise you, it will help you realize some things. Just try it. What do you have to lose? Now stop reading, and I will see you back here in a week. God bless.

TV/Movies

Monday: ____________________
Tuesday: ____________________
Wednesday: ____________________
Thursday: ____________________
Friday: ____________________
Saturday: ____________________

Computer Time (PCs, iPads) Non-Work-Related, (e.g.: Social Media, Internet Surfing, Etc.)

Monday: ____________________
Tuesday: ____________________
Wednesday: ____________________
Thursday: ____________________
Friday: ____________________
Saturday: ____________________

Video Games

Monday: ____________________
Tuesday: ____________________
Wednesday: ____________________
Thursday: ____________________
Friday: ____________________
Saturday: ____________________

Cell Phone Use

Monday: ____________________
Tuesday: ____________________
Wednesday: ____________________
Thursday: ____________________
Friday: ____________________
Saturday: ____________________

Others (Any Electronic Device Not Listed Above)

Monday: ____________________
Tuesday: ____________________
Wednesday: ____________________
Thursday: ____________________
Friday: ____________________
Saturday: ____________________

Total Media in a Week:

Total: ____________

Times by 52 (52 weeks in a year): ________ a year.

This is how much time you waste. Time you could have spent reading books, writing your own novel, going to the gym to get in shape, going back to school, pursing your dreams, chasing passions, finding a wife or husband, working on your marriage, or spending time with your kids and family.

I know what you are thinking. Is this simply Colby's opinion or is it biblical? Can you find this principle in the Bible? Well, let's just look into that question dancing around in your head. Please look at **Ephesians 5:16–17**: "Making the ***best use*** of the time, because the days are evil. Therefore do not be foolish, but understand what the will of the Lord is."

Now can you honestly read this and say watching six hours of TV a night is the best use of your time?

The Holy Spirit opened my eyes to a situation—which I will explain shortly—and after that I noticed that my life had changed for the better.

I had only been back at church about a year or two. I was volunteering and ministering, and I had a very close friend. We used to go to his house after work, sit and watch TV, eat, and then go to bed. That was the routine. I began to observe that this had become an everyday habit. Eventually, things got worse, and I made a decision to stop watching TV and began to read the Bible and journal. I chose to stop because I realized how addicting this routine can become. This source of entertainment allowed us to escape the reality of everyday life. Suddenly, my friend never wanted to leave the house. He stopped going to church, friends' houses, and even family events because he would rather sit on the couch and watch TV. He would turn his phone off on weekends so nobody would bother him, and he would just sit and watch TV all weekend. After a while, his girlfriend left him. Depression began to set in, and he began to complain that there was nothing to do. He had no friends, but he would never want to do anything other than watch TV. I kept an eye for this pattern for a year; it even got to the point where doctors prescribed antidepressants for him. God spoke to me and said that most Americans are doing the same thing. They get out of work and just sit in front of the TV watching other people live their lives, while they waste the gift of life that He has given them. The Holy Spirit showed me that too much TV kills your motivation, desires, creativity, sense of self, sense of purpose, and relationships. You also start to compare yourself to the people you are watching, wondering why you aren't as good as them, why your life is not as good as theirs.

I had a fifty-two-inch flat screen that I gave away. I did not want to be distracted from life anymore. I would read books, pray, go to the gym, take a walk, and write instead of watching TV. I did this for years, and I will be honest, I did not miss having a TV at all. People would talk about shows they watched at work, and when I would tell them that I did not own a TV, they would look at me like I had six heads. I was the odd one because I wanted to enjoy life instead of sit down and watch other people enjoy their lives. Giving away my TV was one of the best things I've ever done.

Let's face facts, people. You only live once and life is short. Most of us spend time thinking of things we have no control over. We spend a lot of energy on this. We spend less time thinking of the things we do have control over: how much TV we watch, how much time we waste, how much time we sleep, what we eat, drink, wear, or what we say. I am telling you that time goes by quickly. If you think you are young and you have all the time in the world, you don't. If you are twenty, you are five years from twenty-five and another five years before thirty. Just keep doing what you are doing and before you know it, you're fifty, saying, "Wow! Just yesterday I was twenty." Everything you do with your life has a consequence. You have a choice, but you cannot choose the results to your choices. We need to stop wasting time. I truly pray that you understand my urgency on this topic. I promise you that on your deathbed, you will not be saying, "Man, I wish I watched more TV," or "I wish I just had more time to play my Xbox." Time is more precious than money; you will never have it again. It's constantly running out. You will never again be the age you are right now ever. You cannot slow time down; it slips through your fingers like sand. When you look back at your life, what do you want to be remembered as? Or be proud of? What do you want your life to produce? More wasted time? I think not. The more time you waste now, the more you will have to play catch up later on in your life. You need to consider the results of your choices now. Think of it this way. Your choices NOW will be your results five years from now. I have said this before.

My pastor, John Carter, asked me this once, "Is God real? Yes or no? It is an either or question. If 'no,' then you better find something to live for. If 'yes,' then you better start spending your time NOW in building a future with God in your life and think of what that is going to look like."

Scriptures

Ephesians 5:16–17

Redeeming the time, because the days are evil.

Colossians 3:23

And whatsoever ye do, do [it] heartily, as to the Lord, and not unto men;

Proverbs 6:9–11

How long wilt thou sleep, O sluggard? When wilt thou arise out of thy sleep?

Ecclesiastes 3:1

To every [thing there is] a season, and a time to every purpose under the heaven.

Proverbs 6:6–8

Go to the ant, thou sluggard; consider her ways, and be wise.

Chapter Fourteen
Amendment 14

Be Creative and Play

Perhaps the most fun of the amendments that God gave me is this one. However, just because it is fun does not make it any less important. This step can be the fuel to our bodies, to our lives. It can get us moving. If we look at it right and put enough thought into this step, it can give us a new passion for life—a passion that drives you and get you out of bed in the morning.

There is something in our spirit that needs to be creative. We all have gifts or ways to be creative, whether it is music, writing, computers, building, cooking, or talking. Whatever your gift is, it inspires you to be creative. You enjoy doing it; it helps you relax and lose yourself. Whatever it is, you need to spend time each day being creative and feeding that desire to create.

Growing up, I loved to write. I wrote short stories, long stories, music, and poetry. I had to write. It motivated me and made me happy. If I stopped writing for a long period of time, I felt worthless. Writing gave me a sense of value and worth. When I wrote, I felt complete. I entered writing competitions and got poems, songs, and short stories published. Writing renewed me;

it made me feel accomplished. If you want to be completely set free in life, then you need to feed that creative side. When I was younger, I used to write every day. Later, when life started to get hectic, I would write less but still at least once a week. When my mom passed way, I stopped writing. I would try to write, but I couldn't; nothing would come out. It was like my mom's death sucked all the creativity out of me. I would sit for hours and stare at a blank piece of paper. Years went by without being creative, without producing something from inside of me that gave me a sense of worth. The less creative I was, the more miserable I became. I had no passion; there's nothing that drove me. Like I said before, creativity gives you fuel.

In the space provided, I want you to list a few ways you can be creative. Take some time out and think of what inspires you. When you figure that out, write it down.

____

____

____

____

Finally, when I began to write again (I literally had to force myself to write), I started to feel set free. God showed me how important being creative is in life. He is a creator; He created us, the world, and the animals by hand. Being creative is a part of God. That is why it is a part of us. We need to create to feel alive and complete. After learning this, I created my personal Constitution—principles to live my life by. One of them is that I am creative and constantly creating new things. This is what it said: "I love to write; it fulfills me. I love to write stories, poetry, sermons, and music. I love to write letters to people; I love to give them encouragement through my writing. I love to write and tell people how I feel about them and that everything will be OK. My best way of communicating is through my writing. I love to create PowerPoint presentations and speeches. Writing brings me more joy than anything else. I have to write. If I am happy, sad, frustrated, lonely, scared, excited, angry, any feeling, writing helps keep my emotions under control. I am at peace and full of joy when I write something new. It's my way of creating something, birthing something from within. I feel that God has given me this gift, and He works through me when I write. I love creating new ideas, concepts, knew ways of dealing with something. I love to share my new creations with people. I love creating new images and logos, new graphics. I love to create new programs, new groups, and new friends. As long as I am creating something, I am happy." Creativity will set you free. This is an important amendment. Follow this and you will find joy and peace in your life.

Now I want you to use my Constitution as an example and write one for yourself about creativity. Trust me, when you go back months or a year later and reread this, it will motivate and inspire you again. I know because it just worked for me.

My Constitution:

____

____

____

____

____

____

The Second Part of This Amendment Is to Play

Sounds simple, right? This may even sound silly or pointless, but I bet that you do not plan fun time. Many times we feel guilty if we are not working or improving or spending time just for "me." Really, challenge yourself and ask, "What do I do for fun? Do I have fun at least once a week?" Many of you would say no. I know. I was once one of these people who never had fun. I was always working, trying to improve, be better. If and only if I finished everything for the week, then maybe I would go do something enjoyable. But I never added "play time" into my weekly planner. Also, watching TV does not count as having fun! Yes, it may be entertaining or relaxing and may even help us shut down at the end of a work day, but for the most part, TV is watching other people live or have fun. I am talking about you going out and doing something fun.

Find time in the day, or at least in the week, to play, relax (not to waste time), and enjoy time with loved ones. Go to the beach, take a walk, play with your kids, go hiking, fishing, boating, swimming, play basketball, and golf—anything that you find fun. This world is full of pressure and pain that we feel as though we have to act serious at all times. Most of us have this "enter at your own risk; beware: do not get too close to me" look on our faces at all times. We have been beaten down so badly in life and hurt so many times that we try to keep people away from us. Even with our own family and friends, there are times when we just want to be left alone and unwind, completely shut out from the world, trying whatever we can to get peace in our mind. This is the time we need to let go and just play. Do something you really and truly love doing—something that brings you joy and happiness, that lets you forget the pressures of life and just allows you to be free. How many of us wish we heard this rule earlier in life? I know I do, because I thought I had to be a grown-up at all times—work, eat, sleep, and work. Then God gave me this step and said, "Have fun. Enjoy life. Take time out of your day or week and schedule play time (fun time)." Find your inner child and have fun. Laugh or do a prank (a harmless one). The Lord will not withhold any good thing.

In the space provided, I want you to brainstorm ways you can have fun. Just start listing ideas:

____

____

____

____

____

____

Now I want you to do something else. This is extremely important. Even if you feel this is very elementary, you will thank me someday for making you do this. I want you to add play and fun into your weekly planner or to-do list on a day when you are either off or have extra time. Write in that space that you will. Starting once a week, try setting a fun day. Now I want you to open your planner on your phone or a paper calendar and write one day per week of playing or having fun for the next month. Block out at least an hour. But if you want to spend a few hours or an entire day having fun, that is fine. Just be sure to make it at least an hour. Write the activity that you are going to do. For example, let's use Saturdays.

Sunday	Monday	Tuesday	Wednesday	Thursday	Friday	Saturday
						10:00 a.m. to 2:00 p.m. play cards with my wife
						10:00 a.m. to 2:00 p.m. go walking in the park

Whatever it is that you enjoy doing, give it a time slot. Do not allow yourself to schedule anything else in its place. If you treat this play time as important, then it will become important. Below you have a monthly calendar. Pick the day, time, and activity for play time and write it in your calendar. Remember, if you write it down and give it a time slot, you will be more likely to actually do it. And if you do this, I promise it will truly set you free.

Fill In Your Play Time:

Sunday	Monday	Tuesday	Wednesday	Thursday	Friday	Saturday

Chapter Fifteen
Conclusion

I pray that not only did you enjoy this book, but that it also changed you. If you continue to follow these amendments and implement them, you will be changed forever. God wants us all to be free. If you have finished this book, you are being set free and that smile you feel on your face is a real smile. That smile is a gift to this world from God. He wants us to enjoy a life with purpose and vision. A life full of love for Him and for others brings true fulfillment. I am so excited for you to start your new life of hope, joy, happiness, and purpose—a life that is on fire for God. This is a new day from this point on. Everything that you have done in your past is forgotten by God; he cannot remember. You are completely set free and able to start over again. That is the beauty and the gift that our Lord Jesus gave to us when He died for us.

Remember a Few Extra Key Points That Will Help You Out in Life

- When you are sinning, you are believing a lie.
- If everything is on the table (all your sins), Satan has no place to hide and expose you.

- If you are bringing glory to yourself, then you are doing something wrong.

Most Important

- Pain, helplessness, defeat, and addiction usually come from lack of love. Lack of self-love or love from family will produce these things in your life. The love of God is the only thing that can break these chains and rip out the root from within you and set you free.
- Everything comes from love. Love is a choice, not a feeling. Feelings come and go, but true love is a decision to stay with it forever.

This book showed you how to have everlasting change in your life. Will you stay with it forever?

I am truly honored and blessed that you read this book. I just want to say thanks.

Contact Me

If you enjoyed this book or have any questions or comments, please go to my web page, *www.sevenmiles.org*, and click ministry, then contact, and leave a note. If you want me to respond to any question or prayer or want to book a speaking event or any other speaking event, please e-mail me at *Colby@sevenmiles.org*.